G000075019

A-Z of ROCK DRUMMERS

HARRY SHAPIRO

PROTEUS

LONDON/NEW YORK

PROTEUS BOOKS is an imprint of
The Proteus Publishing Group

United States
PROTEUS PUBLISHING CO., INC.
733 Third Avenue
New York, NY 10017
distributed by:
THE SCRIBNER BOOK COMPANIES, INC.
597 Fifth Avenue
New York, NY 10017

United Kingdom
PROTEUS (PUBLISHING) LIMITED
Bremar House,
Sale Place
London W2 1PT

ISBN 0 86276 084 4 (paperback)
ISBN 0 86276 085 2 (hardback)

First published in U.S. 1982

First published in U.K. 1982

All photographs by FIN COSTELLO with the exception of the following
colour shots:
Carmine Appice, Paul Cook & Keith Moon/ANDRE CSILLAG; John
Bonham, Phil Collins & Don Henley/CHRIS WALTERS (Photofeatures);

Design: The Acme Art Company
Editor: Kay Rowley
Typset by: SX Composing Ltd.
Printed by: Printer Industria Grafica sa, Barcelona, Spain
D.L.B. 29273 – 1982

INTRODUCTION

Life is full of rhythmic patterns – trains running over railway tracks, waves breaking on beaches; life has its own pulse, scientists talk of biorhythms and without the regular beat of the human heart, there is no life at all. Rhythm is literally within us all. So with music – without the beat there is no life, no celebration, no definition, no heart – we recognise music by its pace and rhythm be it reggae, disco or jazz. Drums are the most basic and oldest instruments known to man used in communication, storytelling, war and ceremony. Since time immemorial people have responded to the primeval pulses symbiotically, feeling the drums rather than hearing them, by ritual movements, tapping feet, waving arms, jiving, twisting, freaking out or pogoing. The innate desire for expression is all-consuming, the urge to move, irresistible.

Yet, despite the fundamental importance of percussion, its craftsmen, its skilled technicians, those who power the engine that drives the train, be it a heavy rock mega-kit or a basic four-piece, are largely ignored. A band really is only as good as its drummer, yet he is the most neglected musician of all. One normally only hears about drummers if they smash up hotel rooms, get arrested, or die. In concert reviews, on album sleeves or in rock reference books he will be mentioned last, if at all. Why should this be? One reason is his relative anonymity on stage, hidden at the back behind a forest of drums, cymbals and mike stands, where he stays for the duration while the guitarist and the vocalist parade out front for the adoring crowds. Drummers are a photographer's nightmare and much of Jim Keltner's delight at the new Simmons electronic kit with flat playing surfaces and lack of metallic spaghetti was expressed as 'Hey, man, they can see me now!'

Another reason is that the population at large don't regard drummers as musicians, least of all rock drummers, because drums themselves are not regarded as musical instruments, just things you hit. 'There's nothing to it' is a common cry until you shove a sceptic behind a kit, thrust a pair of sticks in his hand and tell him to get on with it. Neither

Animal (from The Muppets) nor drum machines have done much to help the image, but they are both new factors serving only to enhance a popular view that is much older. Even though the advent of virtuoso rock drumming in the Sixties brought mass acclaim for the most popular musicians, sometimes they were their own worst enemies indulging in over-long solos calculated to drive all but the most ardent fans straight to the bar.

The struggle for recognition and the nature of drumming itself have tended to make drummers a tribe apart, even in the tight community of musicians. They are a different breed – it can be a lonely business if you are not a top leaguer with your own roadie – arriving first to begin the laborious job of setting up and leaving last when everyone else just has to unplug. It's an esoteric twilight world of tension rods, nut boxes and boom stands to which few are party.

So what follows is a brief introduction to some of the personalities and hidden faces, past and present, their history and those tracks or albums that best demonstrate their skills.

I have used the term 'rock drummer' to indicate those who have operated within rock, however defined, even if rock as such is not their prime area of activity. Thus Tony Williams and Hal Blaine are not rock drummers in the accepted sense, but they have a track record of involvement with rock music. You won't find Elvin Jones or Buddy Rich, but quite obviously the whole illustrious tradition of jazz drumming needs a book to itself. Hopefully, all those drummers most people would expect to find are included, but inevitably personal choice plays a part and I have taken out extra life insurance against sharpened sticks from drummers and fans outraged at particular exclusions. Track and album listings are also selective: session drummers especially have enormous discographies, complicated by the fact that often there are no credit listings for them on many album sleeves.

Finally on the assumption that stick weights, cymbal sizes and drum heads hold a fascination for the dedicated enthusiast only, I have included only general hardware information. In any case, the transitory nature of endorsements, personal preference and the progression of new technology are apt to change these details with frustrating regularity. Top drummers are also likely to have more than one kit for stage and studio work.

I would like to thank the following for their help and co-operation and for the magisterial efforts of some, in the wastelands of rock statistics, whose dedication makes life so much easier: Colin Barratt, John Brady, Phil Defriez, Gerry Evans, Pete Frame, Terry Hounsome, Joe Lung, Alan Merritt, John Tobler, Chris Welch & John Witton.

HARRY SHAPIRO/JULY 1982

Tommy Aldridge

A Tennessee born drummer who first came to public attention with a crude Southern boogie outfit called Black Oak Arkansas. The band had arrived in Los Angeles as Knowbody Else with a Stax label album under its belt, before changing its name to BOA. Aldridge joined them shortly after they signed to Atlantic in 1970. They toured extensively, the stage act revolving around the antics of their extrovert lead singer, Jim Dandy (né Mangrum) resplendent in white fringed buckskin jacket. But Aldridge was not to be denied and his solo *Up* was always one of the high points of the act – he also featured hand drumming à la Bonham. Aldridge left the band in 1976 in a flurry of litigation – apparently trying to leave BOA was harder than getting out of the army: Aldridge has said that he actually wanted to leave the band only a year after joining, but couldn't. From BOA,

he moved to the Pat Travers band replacing Nico McBrain and did a session with Gary Moore. BOA's first UK tour was in 1974 when they made a big impact supporting Black Sabbath. Possibly that connection and a yearning for the ol' fringe jacket up front led Aldridge to join shy, mild-mannered Ozzy Osbourne in Blizzard of Ozz in 1980. Aldridge is one of America's better heavy rock drummers and is less of a showman than in the stick twirling Jim Dandy days. Once quoted as saying 'I don't need thirty tons to play heavy', his large on-stage Sonor drum set-up is nonetheless impressive.

On record
Despite BOA's prolific output and their clutch of gold albums, I personally hesitate to actually recommend anyone *listening* to one of their albums. Instead, bend your ears to Aldridge's work on four Pat Travers albums *Meat in the Street* (1979), *Go For What You Know* (1979), a live album *Crash and Burn* (1980) and *Radio Active* (1981).

Colin Allen

Colin Allen's career goes back to the early Sixties with two bands led by Zoot Money. The first was the Big Roll Band formed in 1963 with Andy Somers of Police fame on guitar and the second, Dantalion's Chariot – same music, but with coloured shirts and lights in a short-lived attempt to capture the psychedelic audience. From there he replaced Jon Hiseman in Mayall's Bluesbreakers with John McVie and Mick Taylor and then

came Stone The Crows.

Guitarist Les Harvey (brother of Alex Harvey) had a band called Power which toured the armed forces bases in Germany. He teamed up with Scots singer Maggie Bell and acquired the services of Led Zeppelin manager Peter Grant, who re-named the band.

They had a hard, punchy soul-based sound, Allen and bassist Jim Dewar underpinning Harvey's excellent guitar work and Maggie Bell's raunchy vocals. Personnel changes nearly split the band in 1971, but the end really came in 1972 when Les Harvey was electrocuted on stage at Swansea University. Peter Green was touted as a replacement, Jimmy McCulloch came in instead but the deserved critical acclaim that the band received was never matched by the commercial success vital for survival and the band folded in 1973.

The superstitious among us would find the deaths of Les Harvey and more recently brother Alex and Jimmy McCulloch and the strangely invisible career of Maggie Bell since 1973, chilling. In fact Colin Allen came out best. He moved on to a totally different musical environment in the shape of Focus, replacing and then being replaced by Pierre van der Linden in 1975 and featured in Mick Taylor's post-Stones touring band of 1977. Currently he is on part-time duty with John Mayall, who is capturing the spirit of '69 with John McVie and Mick Taylor, his main duties being in the service of Rod Stewart as a replacement for Carmine Appice. Colin Allen has also done a number of sessions over the years.

On record
Laurel Canyon John Mayall (1969); *Befour* Brian Auger (1970), *Stone The Crows* (1970), *Ode to John Law* (1970), *Teenage Licks* (1971) & *Continuous Performance* (1972) – all by Stone The Crows, *Why Not?* Ellis (1973), *Aah Laine* Denny Laine (1973), *Hamburger Concerto* (1974), *Ship of Memories* (1974), *Mother Focus* by Focus (1974), *Donovan* Donovan (1977).

Unfortunately, Colin Allen was with Focus during their days of gradual decline as they fumbled around with disco-funk trying to be 'relevant'. His best works on record are the Mayall and Stone The Crows pieces.

Tommy Aldridge

Laurie Allen

Laurie Allen is basically a jazz drummer with a long and illustrious career on the British jazz scene but who has also ventured into the rock field on a number of occasions. He has always been a forward thinking musician interested in new developments – he was a driving force behind the jazz/poetry experiments of the early 1960s, particularly the big band New Departures, including among others, Cream lyricist Pete Brown, saxophonist Dick Heckstall-Smith, Graham Bond and Ginger Baker.

His work in the world of rock has been wide ranging, often collaborating with the more interesting and thoughtful musicians around including Roy Harper, Michael Chapman, Hugh Hopper, Chris Spedding, John Cale, Daevid Allen and Robert Wyatt.

On record

Formerly Fat Harry Formerly Fat Harry (1970), *The Only Lick I Know* Chris Spedding (1972), *The Flying Teapot* Gong (1973), *Rock Bottom* (1974), *Ruth is Stranger than Richard* (1975) by Robert Wyatt.

Jerry Allison

Buddy Holly's school friend from Lubbock, Texas and his drummer in the Crickets throughout all the time they backed him. He also sang accompanying vocals and co-wrote some of the material including Holly's most influential song, *Peggy Sue* which the drummer re-named from its original title *Cindy Sue*.

His drumming was crucial in the overall development of Buddy Holly's music going back to the earliest days when Allison provided the sole accompaniment to the rhythm guitar and vocals. From this came their simplicity and versatility augmented by the addition of bass and rhythm when Buddy switched to lead, thus creating one of the earliest standard white rock'n'roll line-ups. The symbiotic relationship between Allison and Holly comes across in this comment of Allison's from John Goldrosen's excellent biography "– Buddy's guitar playing influenced my drumming more than anything. I haven't played with anyone since that I could play with as well because I learned to play drums with what Buddy played".

When the band came to Britain in 1958, Buddy Holly's Fender Stratocaster caused a sensation but just as many eyes were out on stalks among the drumming fraternity at Jerry Allison's gleaming white Ludwig. The sound of the drums, the cracking snare and the roaring tom toms were a revelation to British drummers, an introduction to what became the Rolls Royce of drum kits; Ludwig snares were *de rigueur* for the Holly-influenced Liverpool sound (Ringo Starr had a gold snare specially made) and later for such rock heavyweights as Ginger Baker and John Bonham.

After Buddy Holly died, the Crickets carried on with a variety of line-ups but always with Jerry Allison on drums. They toured extensively in America and Britain, producing some good material in their own right but unfortunately most fans believed you can't have one without the other. Jerry Allison is now a Texan cattle rancher.

On record

There are numerous compilation albums which contain the essential listening of Buddy Holly and the Crickets included a six album boxed set which appeared in 1979 called *The Complete Buddy Holly*. Recommended listening from the Crickets includes *The Chirpin' Crickets* (1957) and *In Style with Crickets* (1960).

Carmine Appice

Vanilla Fudge sprang to public attention in 1967 with a ponderous but exhilarating cover version of the Supremes hit *You Keep Me Hangin' On*. They played in London at the same time capturing the audiences with their brand of organ-based heavy white funk. Bludgeoned on by the power drumming of Carmine Appice, they caught the attention of many, including John Bonham who took Appice-inspired concepts into Led Zeppelin. The two drummers remained good friends through the years. Fudge music was brave but eventually over-ambitious and tedious and they broke up after five albums for Atco. Appice and bassist tried to form a band in 1969 with Rod Stewart and Jeff Beck, but the guitarist's serious road accident delayed everything for two and a half years, by which time Appice and Bogart formed another heavy outfit with ex-Amboy Dukes vocalist Rusty Day and ex-Mitch Ryder guitarist Jim McCarthy called Cactus and four more albums emerged between 1970-1972. And then came Beck, Bogart and Appice.

One can speculate that if this band had formed when it was supposed to, it would have been enormous – a worthy blues-based power trio successor to Cream. As it was, Jeff Beck was already moving away from this scene and called it a 'Kamikaze operation'. The whole exercise was frustrating for band and fans alike – they left behind a thunderous studio album, an import live album recorded in Japan and a lot of unrealised potential caused mainly by a dearth of good material. One can only ponder on what might have been.

Appice's ill-fortune continued with a short-lived financial disaster called Astrosport in 1974, involving some very fine musicians like guitarist Ray Gomez and bassist Jeff Berlin and KGB with Mike Bloomfield, Ric Grech and Barry Goldberg in 1976. The band was probably doomed from the start by being tagged a 'supergroup' and the end results were a complete waste of time. If the Russians really wanted to undermine American society, then piping the two KGB albums into every home might just do the trick.

Things began to look up when Appice joined the Rod Stewart band and co-wrote the hit single *Do Ya Think I'm Sexy?*, but all was not well. He parted company with the band, to be replaced by Colin Allen. In a recent interview Rod Stewart said 'never trust a drummer with his name on the bass drums' and apparently dubbed Appice 'The Dentist' – too many fill ins! When Appice was stretching out more than was deemed necessary, Stewart would turn round, glare and tap his teeth. Recently Appice has started his own band called the Rockers and has teamed up with the double live gonzo himself, Ted Nugent.

Despite some possibly suspect judgement in the past, or just bad luck, Carmine Appice is nevertheless a damn fine drummer, still pounding his faithful double Ludwig kit, participating in numerous drum clinics and teach-ins, author of one of the best tutors on modern rock drumming and above all, retaining his sense of humour and enthusiasm.

On record

Carmine Appice features on all Vanilla Fudge and Cactus albums, both KGB albums, *KGB* and *Motion* (1976), Rod Stewart's *Footloose and Fancy Free* (1977) and *Blondes Have More*

Vinnie Appice

Fun (1978) and the following sessions: *Eli* Jan Akkerman (1977), *Modern Man* Stanley Clarke (1978), *Ghost Town Parade* Les Dudek (1978).

Recommended is *Beck, Bogart and Appice* (1973) – still a great album particularly *Livin' Alone*.

Vinnie Appice

Carmine's younger brother who has leapt into the limelight from nowhere to take over the drum stool in Black Sabbath recently vacated by Bill Ward. His tight, ferocious sound has added a great deal to Sabbath as can be heard on the latest Sabs album *Mob Rules* (1981). Appice Minor was previously with Rick Derringer playing on three albums, *Derringer* (1976), *Sweet Evil* (1977) and *Live* (1977), the first being particularly fine.

Mick Avory

Mick Avory joined the Kinks when he was 19, he hasn't missed a beat since then, nor is ever likely to until the last curtain comes down on the last rock concert and they finally take his bass drum away. Critics have been less than kind to what has been diplomatically described as Avory's minimalistic approach to drumming. However, there is no denying the tribal rawness of the drums and cymbals that crashed and thumped mercilessly yet precisely through the Kinks heyday of three-chord wonder hits such as *You Really Got Me* (1964), *All Day and All of the Night* (1964), *Till the End of the Day* (1965) and others. Mick Avory's drum sound was an integral part of the power chord rock that the Kinks virtually invented with *You Really Got Me*, a power dissipated in some of the later recorded work but invariably recaptured whenever the band take to the stage. Pye's *Golden Hour of the Kinks Vol.1* (1971) had many of the old hits included and they are all great.

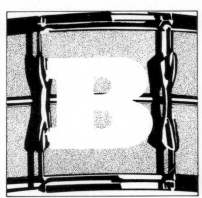

Robbie Bachman

Teamed up with guitarist brother Randy, leader of the successful Guess Who, to form Canada's other successful band, Bachman Turner Overdrive, precursors of today's 'Heavy Pop' favourites like Foreigner. The peak of the band's success came in 1974 with a number one single *You Ain't Seen Nothing Yet*. And we never saw any-

Robbie Bachman

thing afterwards either. Eight albums emerged, *Bachman Turner Overdrive II* (1974) went gold, as did *Four Wheel Drive* (1975), *Not Fragile* (1974) did even better and achieved platinum sales and a *Greatest Hits* album appeared in 1976.

John Badanjek

Probably not a name too familiar to British music fans, but undoubtedly one of the great rock'n'roll drummers. His main band was Mitch Ryder and Detroit Wheels with whom he spent about six years. The first success for the band came in 1965 with a remake of Little Richard's *Jenny Take a Ride* followed up by several other chart successes, in particular *Devil with a Blue Dress On* (1966) and *Sock It To Me* (1967), all dominated by Mitch Ryder's raucous, but stylish vocal sound, a sort of white James Brown and punctuated by Badenjek's red hot stick work. Broken up by internal management wrangling, they reformed in 1971 with a new heavy rock orientation and produced a one-off classic album simply called *Detroit* (1971), very much in the vein of that city's metallic love affair, later promoted on a wider stage by Bob Seger and Ted Nugent.

After Detroit folded, Badenjek took up session work for a coterie of notables, including Edgar Winter, Albert King, Dr. John and Alice Cooper. Since 1977 he has concentrated on his own band, the Rockets, producing three albums to date.

On record
The early Mitch Ryder material is a must, including *Take A Ride* (1966), *Breakout* (1967), *Sock It To Me* (1967), plus *Detroit* (1972). There are various greatest hits albums including one just called *Greatest Hits* (1972) and some recent German imports on the Line label including *How Great My Vacation* (1979) and *Naked But Dead* (1980). John Badenjek can also be heard on: *They Only Come out At Night* Edgar Winter (1973), *Welcome To My Nightmare* Alice Cooper (1975), *Holywood Be Thy Name* Dr. John (1975), *King Albert* Albert King (1977), and all three albums by the Rockets, particularly *Turn Up The Radio* (1979) if you ignore the duff version of *Oh Well*.

Keith Bailey

Keith Bailey is one of rock's 'might

have beens'. In itself, this is nothing out of the ordinary, many musicians have never quite made it. The difference here is that he had the rock world at his feet and walked away.

Brought up in the Swindon area, he was an accomplished player by his mid-teens, drumming with a number of local bands and often joined in jam sessions by Noel Redding who lived nearby. He persuaded the Hendrix management that Keith should be the drummer for the new band but he could not persuade Keith, who felt committed to a band he'd just joined named The Joint. The band, which included Rick Davies, founder member of Supertramp in its ranks, had gigs and film work lined up in Europe. Keith had never heard of Jimi Hendrix, so off he went. After the band came back to England and broke up, Keith was offered the Hendrix gig again, this time because there was a rift in the camp. By now, Keith had certainly heard of Hendrix, but still he said no, because he felt it was the wrong environment for him – a theory of too much too soon, a viewpoint not only remarkably astute and unusual for a 20 year old wanted by the Jimi Hendrix band, but considering the non-careers of Noel Redding and Mitch Mitchell since those heady days, most prophetic. Instead, he teamed up with Graham Bond, who spotlighted him in the act and the word went round 'Bondy's found another Ginger'. When the band folded in 1970 and Bond went to Airforce, the offers for Keith's services flooded in – all the keyboard players wanted him, including Keith Emerson. Eventually, he went with Brian Auger's band for a short time, but became rapicly disillusioned, 'they kept wanting me to put tape on my cymbals'.

Keith felt hemmed in by the musical confines of mainstream rock and spiritual elements too, were entering his life, incompatible with some of the more neanderthal aspects of the music scene. In consequence, he abandoned what could have been a highly lucrative career for the ethereal world of free-form jazz, leading an occasional outfit called Prana, while doing session work for the likes of Keith Tippett and Annette Brox.

On record
The following listing is really all there is: *Annette Brox* Rolling Back (1974), *Keith Tippett* Blue Print (1972), *Warm Dust* Peace For Our Time (1971).

The best of Keith Bailey as a rock drummer is probably the recording

of the John Peel show in 1970, when he was in the Graham Bond Initiation – a blistering solo on the Bond anthem *Wade in the Water*.

Ginger Baker

Without doubt, Peter 'Ginger' Baker is one of the most important heavy rock drummers to have emerged from the welter of virtuosity spawned by the rock boom of the mid-Sixties. At that time, he was a pioneer in all senses of the word; the first to introduce power drumming based on jazz 'feels' into rock, the first to make use of the extended kit, comprising two bass

Ginger Baker

drums and an array of tom-toms, (seven drums being an enormous kit in 1966), and for better or worse, instigator of the drum solo as a climactic, almost obligatory feature in countless successive rock acts.

Like many of the great drummers, Ginger came from jazz. When a taxi flattened his bike and his hopes of becoming a professional bike rider (immortalised in the album title *Disraeli Gears*), he discovered another talent, bluffed his way on to the trad scene of the late Fifties, played with everyone, argued with them all and made his recording debut on Terry Lightfoot's *Tradition in Colour* album in 1958. From there, he followed time

honoured paths around the London jazz club circuit, until his fateful meeting with Jack Bruce, Graham Bond and Dick Heckstall-Smith in the John Burch Octet (1962).

But jazz was dying and R&B was the up and coming mode so they switched allegiance to the seminal Blues Incorporated led by Alexis Korner. Within this band, however, Ginger, Jack and Graham started playing separate gigs during the intervals and at different venues when the Blues Incorporated wasn't playing, featuring Graham's Hammond organ rather than Alexis' horn line-up. This led to a split in 1963 and the formation of the legendary Graham Bond Orga-

nisation, adding a young unknown guitarist called John McLaughlin; saxophonist Dick Heckstall-Smith joined later – it was the genesis of jazz-rock as it became known.

Ginger and Jack quickly built up a reputation as the best rhythm section in Europe, Ginger in particular leaving audiences and other musicians alike, open-mouthed at his confident polyrhythmic pyrotechnics executed mainly on a basic four drum kit. Unfortunately the band, for all its raw power and skill, could not match the wider appeal of the clean cut Liverpool sound – they had no hit records, money was tight and Ginger was restless.

Around April 1966, he met up with Eric Clapton, similarly dissatisfied with his current John Mayall gig and they brought in Jack Bruce, who had been with Mayall and then Manfred Mann since leaving the Bond band some six months earlier. They got together in Ginger's Neasden house, played 'something in D' for several hours and as they say, the rest is history. Cream was born. After initial stumblings in this country, Cream conquered America – the right band in the right place at the right time and individually they became household names, winning music polls year after year. If every guitarist wanted to be Eric Clapton, every drummer wanted to be Ginger Baker. Yet despite all their success, the band went stale, bogged down in the long improvisation format they had created and in 1968 they called it a day, after a historic farewell concert at the Albert Hall.

To a certain extent, Ginger was reverting musically back to the days of the earliest jazz drummers who emphasised the bass drum over the cymbal, unlike the bop drummers of the Fifties. Taking ideas from his mentor, the late and very great Phil Seaman, Ginger used one and then two bass drums to anchor down a sound that rapidly metamorphosed from jazz to rock. *Toad*, climax of the Cream stage act, was often over-indulgent, anything up to half an hour, but unlike many subsequent tub thumping excesses, his solos were always lyrical, a quality they retain today, recalling the style of Max Roach. You could almost sing the solo with its cascading rolling triplets, a reflection of the influence of African drum sounds on Ginger's playing, even before his Nigerian sojourn, with their vocal intonations and symbolisms – the drums that speak.

After Cream, Ginger's career was very patchy. The over-hyped but eventually underrated Blind Faith, came and went, to be followed by Ginger's personal baby, Airforce in 1970. A juggernaut of a band, top heavy with personalities like Steve Winwood, Denny Laine and Graham Bond and overbalanced by sheer weight of numbers, up to thirteen at one point. It was just too unwieldy; one night magic, the next a disasterous mess but an ambitious project for which Ginger deserved more credit than he got.

It is tragic that since 1971, a musician with so much to offer, has done so

little. The grounding of Airforce needed a long period of convalesence but he seemed unable to escape many of the business and personal problems that have dogged his career, underlined by doubtful enterprises involving polo ponies in Britain and a recording studio in Nigeria. His musical excursions have been equally unsuccessful – the Baker Gurvitz Army, who put out one reasonable album and two dogs, the whole episode a forbidden topic of conversation, Energy, now defunct and two farcically rapid associations with the revamped Atomic Rooster and Hawkwind. It must be said that his temperament does nothing to help; it seems neither can he keep his own bands together, nor work within the confines of someone else's. But as a drummer, he remains a virtuoso, not a great technician in the Cobham sense, but a 'Guvnor' drummer nevertheless – with the coming of Ginger Baker, they broke the mould.

Recommended Listening
The best of Baker is to be found on the two Graham Bond Organisation albums, *Sounds Of '65* and *There's A Bond Between Us* (1966). On Cream and other albums, Ginger was largely embellishing the basic themes and ideas laid down on these albums. Of particular note are the solos, *Oh Baby* on the first and *Camels and Elephants* on the second which coalesced to form the seminal drum solo *Toad* on *Wheels of Fire*. Also worth hearing, is the later Organisation double *Solid Bond* (1970, but re-released since) and the brushwork on *Traintime* also from the *Wheels of Fire* Cream album. On all his records and on stage, he plays Ludwig drums, "I'd never play anything else".

John Barbata

The arrival of John Barbata into Jefferson Starship epitomised the change from the more experimental Airplane days of *Bless Its Pointed Head*, to the more tightly disciplined and commercial approach of *Dragonfly* and *Red Octopus*.

After a series of high school bands, Barbata's leap into the big time came with the Turtles, at their height when he joined them in 1966. From there he went on tour with the Everlys, replaced Dallas Taylor in Crosby, Stills, Nash and Young and Russ Kunkel in Neil Young's short-lived Stray Gators, before linking up with Jefferson Airplane during their transitionary 1972-

1974 period. He himself was replaced around 1979 by Aynsley Dunbar.
On record
During his CSNY days, he appeared on their collective album *Four Way Street* (1972) as well as their individual solo efforts; Neil Young *Time Fades Away* (1973), *Stephen Stills* (1970); Graham Nash's *Songs for Beginners* (1971) and *Wild Tales* (1973). He also featured on Grace Slick's *Manhole* (1974) and the Kantner/Slick collaboration *Baron Von Tolbooth* (1973). Among many other sessions have included Davon Mason's best album *Alone Together* (1970) and John Sebastian. Recommended are the more recent Starship albums, *Dragonfly* (1974) and *Red Octopus* (1975).

Barriemore Barlow

Took over from Clive Bunker in Jethro Tull after *Aqualung* (1971) and stayed with the band up to the *Stormwatch* album (1979). He now backs a promising outfit (on paper at any rate), called Tandoori Cassette featuring Zal Cleminson, Ronnie Leahy and Charlie Tumahai.
On record
An unusual drummer in some respects in that despite possessing the classic heavy rock double Ludwig during Tull days, and all that implies, he handled very deftly Ian Anderson's often tricky pastoral arrangements which were a fusion of folk and rock without being folk/rock in the traditional Fairport Convention meaning of the term. The best examples of this are *Minstrel in the Gallery* (1975) and *Songs from the Wood* (1977). That Barlow seems at home in a number of softer environments is demonstrated by his touring with Richard Digance and his appearance on Maddy Prior's *Woman in the Wings* album (1978).

Frank Beard

Anchor man of a phenomenally successful three piece Texan boogie band called ZZ Top and the only one without a Methuselah beard! ZZ Top broke attendance records all over the place between 1974-76, once topping the bill over Bad Company and Santana. Then they disappeared

Brian Bennett

14

completely, re-emerging with two archetypal genre-albums – *Deguello* (1979) and *El Loco* (1981), one of the years' nice surprises.

On record

Both albums mentioned here are recommended as is *Fandango* (1975), half studio and half live, containing their anthem *Thunderbird*. Courtesy of some excellent production, particularly on *El Loco*, prominence is given to Beard's simple but effective backbeats and the full fat sound essential for any power trio.

Fred Below

One of the world's best blues drummers and as Chess Records' house drummer has played with all the great Chess artists like Eddie Boyd, Buddy Guy, Howlin' Wolf, Little Walter, Otis Rush, Muddy Waters and Sonny Boy Williamson. Another major Chess recording artist was one Chuck Berry and Fred Below is to be heard on many of the definitive Chuck Berry Chess sessions, although with record companies' unwillingness to list musicians on anthology albums, it is not possible to identify precisely which ones. Nowadays, the versatile drummer has a jazz group in Chicago.

Brian Bennett

The Brian Bennett story begins in the 2 I's coffee bar in London's West End during the late Fifties, where musicians met up and bands (or groups as they were called in those days – bands meant Joe Loss and the music that mum liked) were formed. Bennett teamed up with Hamburg-star-to-be, Tony Sheridan and backed Conway Twitty on OH BOY, a seminal British TV rock'n'roll show. From there, he featured in the support groups of major British pop idols like Marty Wilde and Tommy Steele, gaining much respect as a top class drummer with every gig he played.

In 1961 he became the third drummer to join the Shadows, following in the footsteps of Tony Meehan and Tony Smart. The line-up of Marvin, Welch, Farrar and Bennett lasted for ten years, by which time Bennett had staked a claim in the pantheon of great British drummers, noted for being a master technician without being flashy or robotic. After the Shadows broke up, he went into production, was much in demand as a ses-

sion musician, recorded solo albums and occasionally appeared in various revitalisations of Georgie Fame and the Blue Flames. Then came the dramatic Shadows revival of the mid Seventies, which continues unabated.

On record

Probably his most influential piece as far as British drummers were concerned was his *Little B* solo on *Out Of The Shadows* (1962). *Change of Direction* (1968), *The Illustrated London Pride* (1969), *Rock Dreams* (1977) and *Voyage* (1978) represent his solo output and among his many sessions are Chris Spedding (1976), Sutherland Brothers' *Down to Earth* (1977) and The Walker Brothers' *Lines* (1976).

Ron Berg

A good, down-the-line no messing British rock drummer, who first appeared on the scene with Blodwyn Pig in 1968, the band formed by current insurance salesman Mick Abrahams, after leaving Jethro Tull. When Pig broke up, he featured on Savoy Brown, Juicy Lucy and Alvin Lee sessions. More recently, he teamed up with ex-Blodwyn Pig bassist Andy Pyle in United, renamed Network.

On record

Ron Berg plays on both fine Blodwyn Pig albums, *Ahead Rings Out* (1969) and *Getting To This* (1970), *See My Way* and *Drive Me* on the latter album being typical of his approach. Other sessions: *Pieces* Juicy Lucy (1972), *Jack the Toad* Savoy Brown (1973), *Pump Iron* Alvin Lee (1975).

Bev Bevan

ELO's Bev Bevan and guitarist Denny Laine started their music careers together in 1962 by forming Denny Laine and the Diplomats, part of the burgeoning Midland scene that spawned such bands as the Moody Blues, Wizzard, the Idle Race and one of the Led Zeppelin precursors, Band of Joy. DL and the Diplomats resplendent in silver suits, recorded much, released nothing and broke up around 1964. Bevan went immediately on the German club circuit with Carl Wayne and the Vikings which metamorphosed into the Move (1966-71) and then split into Wizzard and ELO, who after many trials and tribulations finally made it to superstardom.

Interestingly, Bevan was using a double bass drum kit back in Diplomat days, which may just have preceded its use by Ginger Baker and Keith Moon. The kit then was a Ludwig, but since 1969 Bevan has been loyal to Slingerland, although he has dropped the second bass drum. An unpretentious drummer who knows his job within the structure of a band like ELO, with a high degree of musical discipline.

On record

Any Move compilation will demonstrate the loud but controlled drumming that Bevan took with him to ELO, particularly singles like *Flowers In The Rain* (1967) and *Blackberry Way* (1969). ELO's *On The Third Day* (1973) and *Out Of The Blue* (1977) chronicle how the Bevan style is integrated into Jeff Lynne's tight orchestral arrangements.

Dave Bidwell

Dave Bidwell whacked out dem ol' 4/4 blues for two bands in the vanguard of the late Sixties British blues boom – Chicken Shack and Savoy Brown, who he joined after Chicken Shack broke up for the first of many times. He was with Savoy Brown during the latter part of their American successes which contrasted with band's 'cult following' back home.

On record

Forty Blue Fingers (1968), *O.K. Ken* (1968), *100 Ton Chicken* (1969) & *Accept* (1970) – all by Chicken Shack, *Street Corner Talking* (1970), *Hellbound* (1972), *Lions Share* (1973) & *Jack the Toad* (1973) – all by Savoy Brown.

He also featured (along with every other British blues musician who ever drew breath) on the Martha Velez album *Fiends and Angels* (1969).

Jimmy Carl Black

The Soul Giants were formed by Jimmy Carl Black and Roy Estrada with the idea of playing R&B. This they continued to do, even after Frank Zappa joined, but Frank had other ideas as they were soon to find out. What Zappa had in mind became the tumbling anarchic juggernaut known as the Mothers of Invention, which he rigidly controlled from its inception.

Bev Bevan

Black remained Zappa's number one drummer through the early personnel changes the band went through, up to the recording of the second album *Absolutely Free* (1967). For this session, Black switched to percussion, moving over for Billy Mundi, and he remained in that capacity until Zappa broke the band up for the first time in 1969. Although he appeared on *200 Motels* (1971), Jimmy Black had already formed Geronimo Black with Roy Estrada, the name being in recognition of Black's Indian heritage. By the time the band broke up Black had already moved to New Mexico where he recorded an album of fifties rock'n'roll tracks. Some of these turn up on a recently released album called *Grand Mothers* (1982), an anthology of previously unreleased recordings by ex-Mothers members. Black also supplied vocals on *Joe's Garage* (1980).

On record

Freak Out (1966), *Absolutely Free* (1967), *We're Only In It For The Money* (1967), *Lumpy Gravy* (1967), *Cruisin' With Ruben And The Jets* (1968), *Mother Mania* (1969), *Uncle Meat* (1969), *Weasels Ripped My Flesh* (1970), *Burnt Weeny Sandwich* (1970), *200 Motels* (1971), *Joe's Garage* (1980) – all by Frank Zappa/ Mothers of Invention, *Geronimo Black* (1972), *Welcome Back Geronimo Black* (1973).

Chuck Blackwell

Session drummer with Shelter Records' stable connections who has contributed some nicely understated rock rhythms to the following urban and country blues oriented albums: *Taj Mahal* (1967), *Natch'l Blues* (1968 – spoilt by bad production) & *Giant Step* (1969) by Taj Mahal, *Getting Ready* (1971), *Texas Cannonball* (1972), *Woman Across The Water* (1973) by Freddie King, *Jesse Ed Davis* (1971), *Carney* (1972), *Stop All That Jazz* (1974) by Leon Russell.

He was also with a band called Colours, with the late Carl Radle on bass, which released two albums in the Seventies.

Hal Blaine

Top dog in the exclusive brethren of session drummers – joined in recent years by Steve Gadd, Blaine's only equal in versatility and wide ranging experience.

After touring in the Fifties with Tommy Sands and Patty Page, Hal Blaine got into session work on the West Coast around 1961, already a musician of some twenty years standing. He backed The Crystals on *He's a Rebel* and from that became a regular member of Phil Spector's session crew, which included Leon Russell, Barney Kessell and Sonny Bono. It was due to Phil Spector encouraging Blaine to stretch out, that he made his definitive statements on record, *Be My Baby* by the Ronettes and the Crystals' *Da Doo Ron Ron*. If he'd done nothing else, this would have been enough to warrant a place in the annals of great drum tracks. What Blaine added to the famous multilayered Spector sound, was a biting drum attack, using a 12 drum kit, unheard of in studios used to handling a four piece. The Spector technique made twelve drums sound like twelve hundred. Since becoming a session drummer, he has only done two touring stints – one with Nancy Sinatra (featuring on his umpteenth hit single *These Boots Were Made For Walking*) and with John Denver, agreeing to be his road drummer back in 1974.

His kit in the early Sixties was a Ludwig and he's been with them ever since, despite the inevitable enticements from other companies, using his much beloved blue sparkle kit and 36-year-old Zildjian cymbals.

On record

Hal Blaine has recorded with the Beach Boys, Elvis Presley, Frank Sinatra, Frank Zappa, the Mamas and the Papas, the Everly Brothers, Bobby Darin, George Harrison, John Lennon and Wings among countless others, plus TV and film scores and over 300 jingles. It is likely that somewhere in America, Hal Blaine is heard on TV most nights of the week.

Some of his rock sessions have included: *Surf City* Jan and Dean (1963), *Love Is The Law* Graham Bond (1969), (an interesting album this, with Bond doing all other instrumentation and vocals. Of note is the track *Our Love Will Come Shining Through* for tight jazzy inter-play between organ and drums without any holes in the sound despite the presence of only two

musicians. Unfortunately, through half-baked corporate thinking, this album was never released in Britain). *Angel Clare* Art Garfunkel (1973), *Mother And Child Reunion* Paul Simon (1972), *The Graduate* Simon and Garfunkel (1970), *Roger McGuinn* (1973), *Katy Lied* Steely Dan (1975), *Live and Learn* Elkie Brooks (1979).

John Bonham

For a band that had suffered so much personal tragedy, the death in September 1980 of Led Zeppelin's John Bonham was the final blow – they just couldn't carry on without him. Fortunately, the memory of John Bonham has remained relatively unbesmirched by gutter press revelations about his gregarious off-stage life, a fate from which Keith Moon has not been spared. This is gratifying from many points of view, not least of which is the fact that Led Zeppelin not only lost a close and valued friend, but one of the greatest heavy rock drummers of all time.

Although he would never have called himself a technician, he was master of the syncopated hypnotic rock steady rhythm, the inspirational use of crash cymbal for emphasis and attack, and owner of the meanest right foot in the business – witness those stunning triplet bass drum patterns on *Good Times, Bad Times*. His value to Led Zeppelin and rock music was inestimable and, as their breakup underlined, what he brought to the band was irreplaceable.

John Bonham's biography is fairly straightforward – a succession of long forgotten early Sixties bands, the Way of Life, Steve Brett and the Mavericks, Terry and the Spiders and with Robert Plant in Birmingham, the Band of Joy and Crawling King Snakes. Jimmy Page wanted B. J. Wilson of Procul Harum in his new band, formed after the Yardbirds broke up but Robert Plant persuaded him otherwise. His impact was immediate – a drummer of great precision and control, knowing precisely where to be busy and where to be the steady platform, but also skilful and possessed of enormous strength even though he was not really hitting the drums harder than anyone else. Drum tuning was one factor, a very penetrating, booming sound which hundreds of other drummers frantically tried to copy. But probably the main reason why Bonham cut through so well was, despite the fact that Led Zeppelin were a heavy rock band, Jimmy Page's guitar sound was thin, rather than gutsy, with lots of power chords and the bass was way down in the registers, muted and unobtrusive. When Bonzo got into the driving seat, he just took off, there was nothing in the way of his thunderous sound using the over-sized Ludwig drums he pioneered. It would be impossible to pick out the best of Bonham on record, everything he did was magisterial, although he wisely cut out his extended soloing on stage, which often became just plain boring. One might just mention the tumultuous re-entry into the main theme of *Whole Lotta Love* after the electronic passage, the almost unbearable tension leading up to his entry on *Stairway To Heaven, Dazed and Confused, Misty Mountain Hop, Custard Pie, Communications Breakdown, Kashmir, When The Levee Breaks* and possibly his ultimate statement, the intro to *Rock And Roll*.

A John Bonham performance was once described as "the aural equivalent of watching Clint Eastwood club eight bad guys over the head with a two-by-four, while driving a derailed locomotive through their hideout". In other words, he was a killer, the likes of which will probably never be seen again.

John Boudreaux

Top New Orleans drummer whose sessions have included work for Professor Longhair and *Sun Moon and Herbs* (1971), *Hollywood Be Thy Name* (1975) by Dr. John, *Maria Muldaur* (1974), *Triumvirate* Mike Bloomfield (1973), *Ghost Writer* Garland Jeffreys (1977).

Terry Bozzio

An exceptionally talented young drummer, well schooled in symphonic and jazz percussion and high-energy rock.

He started out a jazz drummer hooked on the demonic style of Tony Williams but earning his bread during 1973 in the orchestra pit of the rock musical GODSPELL. His sojourn with Latin-funk band Azteca was short-lived largely because Tony Williams' pyrotechnics and commercially-sounding backbeats don't mix.

The turning point for Bozzio came when he passed an audition for the awesome Frank Zappa and embarked on just about the toughest musical education imaginable. Zappa has a reputation for pushing his musicians to their limits and then some, writing increasingly complex material as if to say 'right, lads, try that one for size'. To contradict a Zappa album One Size *doesn't* fit all and many have fallen by the wayside, defeated by Zappa's strict working discipline and musical complexities but Terry Bozzio came through to become one of Zappa's premier percussionists.

In between his Zappa work, he toured with the Brecker Brothers and almost joined Thin Lizzy, until he met up with new Zappa recruit, keyboardist Eddie Jobson formerly with Roxy Music. Their friendship blossomed and Bozzio followed Jobson into UK after the departure of Bill Bruford and Alan Holdsworth in 1979. In some respects both versions of UK were playing rather dated material, however expertly executed but the audiences loved it and they toured extensively. However, egos loomed large and the band's second line-up folded after two albums. Since then, Terry Bozzio has been involved with his own LA based band, Missing Persons.

In his move away from jazz, he has largely eschewed heavy use of cymbals and their sparse use is one of the features of his style, preferring to rely on hi-hat/drum syncopations. On the hardware side, he has been using a mixture of Tama drums and rototoms with Paiste cymbals.

On record

His recorded work with Zappa includes *Bongo Fury* (1975), *Zoot Allures* (1976), *Sheik Yerbouti* (1979) and *Live in New York* (1978) which features a track called *The Black Page*, one of the most breathtakingly complex pieces of drum music that Zappa has ever written and a marvellous testament to his drummer's abilities. There was a spate of albums put out around this time like *Studio Tan* (1978) which Zappa disowned. They have few, if any, musician credits, but it is likely that Terry Bozzio is featured.

He also plays on the second UK album *Danger Money* (1979) and the live *Night After Night* (1979). Particularly noteworthy are the fill-ins and pattern changes on *The Only Thing She Needs* from *Danger Money*. Even on this relatively limited recorded output, all the signs are that Bozzio will go from strength to strength.

Geoff Britton

British drummer who has moved in and out of the limelight over the years. He played with East of Eden when this jazzy Eastern influenced band was a very popular club attraction, especially in France around 1969-1970. He was with the Wild Angels and appeared on Danny Kirwan's solo album *Second Chapter* (1975) before shooting into the headlines by joining Wings. However, *his* wings were clipped only nine months after joining when on the band's second recording trip to America, he was sacked in favour of Joe English. Even worse was to follow for him with two quasi-supergroups, Rough Diamond and its successor, Champion. The first band contained ex-Uriah Heep vocalist David Byron and guitar maestro Clem Clempson; the second saw Clempson gamely soldiering on. Both bands released an album each in 1977 and 1978 respectively, planned tours that never happened, had management hassles and then found themselves labelled has-beens when the new wave moved in. More recently, Geoff Britton has appeared on the Earthband's album *Angel Station* (1979).

Bill Bruford

As one of Britain's most technically accomplished and intelligent percussionists, Bill Bruford has always adopted a thoroughly uncompromising attitude to his music, never afraid to leave commercially successful ventures in pursuit of his fearsomely high standards and expectations.

His first taste of success came in Yes, with its original line-up of Jon Anderson, Peter Banks, Tony Kaye and Chris Squire and Bruford who through five Yes albums supplied the most supple and imaginative drumming. But he was unhappy with the band, mainly because he felt that the arrangements were too inflexible and over-rehearsed, lacking the framework of free-ranging fluidity within which Bruford now felt he wanted to play. His dissatisfaction coupled with the chance to enhance his own experience as a drummer and make progress, led him to accept Robert Fripp's offer of the job in King Crimson, particularly as it would give him the opportunity to play with a percussionist he had long admired, Jamie Muir.

King Crimson's 1972 lineup of Bruford, Muir, Fripp, John Wetton and violinist/keyboardist David Cross, was in retrospect, the most talented team that Fripp ever assembled, producing classic albums of taut controlled aggression, stylistically Crimson's finest work. On stage they were a revelation, British virtuoso musicianship at its most inspired, even though they lost the eccentric Muir early on. When Fripp broke up the band in 1974, he said "King Crimson is completely over for ever and ever". Well, you may have noticed that they are not – Fripp reformed the band in 1981, with Bruford and they released the excellent *Discipline* (1981) and *Beat* (1982).

But this is leaping ahead. After 1974, Bruford, for a long while now recognised as a major force in drumming, went into session work and touring with a variety of bands, including Gong and Roy Harper. He joined National Health in 1975 and spent some time helping out Phil Collins on the road with Genesis in 1976. In a sense, National Health was a stereotyped Bruford vehicle, according to his professional philosophies – challenging, free flowing jazz-oriented progressive rock, lots of invention and skill, but sacrificing commercial viability in the process.

Bruford's next major commitment was UK with Eddie Jobson, John Wetton and guitarist Allan Holdsworth. Despite the range and depth of talents on show (or possibly because of them), this was a troubled band from the start. It soon became clear that, while Jobson and Wetton wanted to play the sort of accessible, simplistic rock that would fill arenas and sell albums, this was anathema to Bruford and Holdsworth, neither of whom was willing to compromise their own personal benchmarks of professional motivation. Their one album contained many fine moments but on stage, the whole exercise was sterile and emotionless, four musicians playing for themselves.

Inevitably, Bruford struck out on his own, named his band after himself and did it his way, with gifted musicians like Dave Stewart and bassist Jeff Berlin. Four albums have been released so far, the most musically successful being *Gradually Going Tornado* (1979), strongly thematic, superbly produced, displaying the seamless rhythmic flow with sparse use of cymbals that characterises

Bruford's work. A Ludwig player, Bruford has played rototoms and more recently, the eight-ply maple shell drums from the Denver based firm Dragon. One of the men who, along with Phil Collins, liberated drumming from the age of gaffer tape and blankets, Bruford's brilliance remains undiminished – the effortless brutality with which he sets about a kit as potent in Crimson '82 as it was with Crimson '72.

On record
*Particularly recommended
Yes (1969), *Time and A Word* (1970), *The Yes Album* (1971), *Fragile* (1971) & *Close To The Edge* (1972) all by Yes, *Larks Tongue In Aspic* (1973), *Starless and Bible Black* (1974), *Red* (1974), *USA* (1975) & *Discipline* (1981) all by King Crimson, *H.Q.* Roy Harper (1975), *Beginnings* (1977) & *Steve Howe Album* (1979) by Steve Howe, *Fish Out Of Water* Chris Squire (1975), *Six Wives of Henry VIII* Rick Wakeman (1973), *Sound Of The Bell* Pavlov's Dog (1976 – a weird outfit this – melodic, progressive rock, with a vocalist who came across as an amalgam of Tiny Tim, Captain Beefheart and Roger Chapman. Other musicians on this album included Elliott Randall, Michael Brecker, Andy Mackay and the High Wycombe Boys Choir!), *Feels Good To Me* (1978), *Bruford* (1979), *Bruford Tapes* (1979) & *Gradually Going Tornado* (1979) all by Bruford.

Clive Bunker

Clive Bunker's biggest claim to fame was his stint with Jethro Tull from the band's formation in 1968 up to 1971 when, to the complete surprise and disappointment of his many fans, he quit the band that was taking the world by storm.

He moved on to an ill-fated enterprise called Jude with Robin Trower and vocalist Frankie Miller. Since then, his career has been a mixture of solid album work but less successful live outings. During the mid-Seventies, Mick Abrahams tried to reform Blodwyn Pig and brought Bunker in on drums. Their live gigs were quite enjoyable, Bunker as interesting and inventive as ever within conventional rock idioms but the band was inevitably short-lived. He went on the road with Steve Hillage and Gordon Giltrap and joined Alan White and Bill Bruford as the third

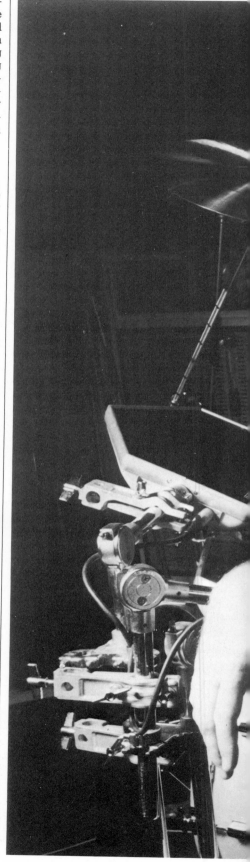

Bill Bruford

drummer on Steve Howe's second album (1979). In addition, he formed a band called Aviator with ace wind instrumentalist Jack Lancaster and former Earthband guitarist Mick Rogers. Unfortunately the material was sub-standard and their two albums did not match up to the promise of the band on their individual past records.

On record

Jethro Tull, even in the earliest days, were not a straight forward rock band, their work being shot through with all kinds of interesting light and shade involving jazz and folk forms as well as hard-driving blues-rock. This is amply demonstrated by their first two definitive albums *This Was* (1968) and *Stand Up* (1969), which along with the retrospective and part-live *Living in the Past* (1971) showcase some of their best music. Bunker was equally at home with the riff-based *Cat Squirrel* or the out and out jazz feels of Roland Kirk's *Serenade To A Cuckoo* both on *This Was*, the album that also featured his solo outing and highlight of the live act, *Dharma For One*. The solo had flair and even humour, the more so for being executed on a small kit. It re-appears in live form on *Living In The Past* but, despite a marvellous intro, seems to lack ideas relying too heavily on Baker-inspired tom tom and bass drum patterns. Bunker's overall versatility was carried on through to his other recorded work, including Gordon Giltrap's *Fear Of The Dark* (1978) and the Steve Hillage live album *Live Herald* (1978).

Richard Burgess

Landscape drummer Richard Burgess, has been in the vanguard of those percussionists making extensive use of electronic drums and similar hardware, which have become so prominent in contemporary music in recent years. Very much the publicist of the 'new wave' of percussion, Burgess had advocated its use primarily to free the drummer from boring beat work. Landscape was formed about six years ago as an *avant-garde* jazz group, which has now switched its attention to more commercial areas with singles like *Einstein-a-go-go*. A very visible acoustic drummer, Burgess manages to project his personality through the drums which are always very loud in the mix. On *Landscape* (1979), the Pearl bass drums are mixed either side of centre, so intriguing cross-rhythms dance from one speaker to the other.

A very versatile musician, Burgess produces Spandau Ballet and was in on the design stage of the Simmons SDS5 touch sensitive electronic drum kit, one of the biggest innovations in drum hardware for many years and currently the centre of much interest around the world (see also DRUMKITS).

A regular contributor to magazines, few drummers around have such a technical grasp of the new innovations in percussion and their potential as Richard Burgess.

Kenny Buttrey

Nashville's most famous and most accomplished session drummer called upon by numerous artists when country inspired rhythms are required; delicate hi-hat snaps and superbly understated brush patterns. The listing of some of his sessions below, will give a good idea of the range of classic albums that sport his talents. In common with many session musicians, Buttrey has played with few bands in any regular capacity. Session work and touring require different temperaments but occasionally session musicians who play frequently together will form a loose association, release some material and even play a few gigs.

One such association was Area Code 615, a group of highly respected Nashville session musicians, including ace harp player Charlie McCoy. Although never intended to be a working band, their first album just called *Area Code 615* (1969) was sufficiently well received to stimulate a follow-up *Trip in the Country* (1970). The band's lasting legacy was a track called *Stone Fox Chase*, since 1971 the theme music for BBC-TV's rock programme THE OLD GREY WHISTLE TEST. Other Buttrey touring gigs have included a miserable Neil Young experiment called Stray Gators and a successful tour to France with Billy Swan in 1973 and 1975 respectively.

On record

Starred items are particularly recommended.

Blonde on Blonde (1966), *John Wesley Harding* (1968), *Nashville Skyline* (1969) primarily *Lay Lady Lay, Self Portrait* (1970). (Nashville's finest at their finest, the musicians doing ample justice to the comprehensiveness of Dylan's emotional range, demonstrated on the first two albums listed; anthems of hard cynicism and soft focus). *Really (superb production – 1972), *Troubadour* (1976), *5* (1979), *Grasshopper* (1982) all J. J. Cale.

The ideal drummer for the musician who epitomises that well-worn phrase 'laid-back'.

Home Free (1973), *Netherlands* (1977) & *Phoenix* (1980) Dan Fogelberg, *Mudlark* Leo Kottke (1971), *Balance* (1979), *Harpin' The Blues* (1970), *Nashville Hit Man* (1974), *Play It Again Charlie* (1976) & *Country Cookin'* (1977) all by Charlie McCoy, *California Bloodlines* John Stewart (1969 – recorded across the street at the same time as Nashville Skyline, you probably couldn't see Buttrey for Texan dust. John Stewart's best album.) *Willard* (1970), *Live In The Wind* (1977), *Harvest* (1972) & *Tonight's The Night* (1975) by Neil Young, *David's Album* Joan Baez (1969), *Ladies Love Outlaws* Waylon Jennings (1971), *Jesus Was A Capricorn* Kris Kristofferson (1973), *Gord's Gold* Gordon Lightfoot (1975), *Go For Broke* Matthew's Southern Comfort (1976).

Kenny Buttrey has also done sessions for Elvis Presley, the Pointer Sisters, Manhattan Transfer, Donovan and Splinter and his harder rock orientated work has included the Steve Miller back-up band for Chuck Berry and *Cristo Redentor* Harvey Handel (1968), *Rock'n'Roll Resurrection* Ronnie Hawkins (1972), *Seven* Bob Seger (1974).

Bobby Caldwell

A relatively obscure American drummer worth including on the strength of his powerhouse drumming on *Johnny Winter And Live* (1971) – notably on *Good Mornin' Little Schoolgirl* – among one of the best live albums ever recorded. He was one of the original members of Johnny Winter's backup band from 1970-1972 and also appeared on Winter's *Saints and Sinners* album (1973). His next venture was an outfit called Captain Beyond, lining up with ex-Deep Purple vocalist Rod Evans and two former members of Iron Butterfly, Larry "Rhino" Rheinhart and Lee Dorman. Despite some tasty heavy rock playing and a 3-D concept on the first album cover, the band fizzled out, trying again in 1977 to little effect. In the meantime, Caldwell teamed up with Keith Relf in Armageddon and went on to record a solo album playing bass, guitar and keyboards.

On record

Apart from his Johnny Winter sessions: *Captain Beyond* (1972) & *Sufficiently Breathless* (1973) by Captain Beyond, *Armageddon* (1975), *Bobby Caldwell* (1978).

Jim Capaldi

As well as being Traffic's fine drummer, Jim Capaldi has been a force to reckon with as a songwriter and vocalist.

Traffic were formed in 1967 after Stevie Winwood left the Spencer Davis Group, moving to a cottage in Berkshire and starting a fashion in British rock known as 'getting it together in the country', which fast became a cliché along the lines of "the split was due to musical differences" (meaning "we were musical and he was different"). However, unlike some groups, Traffic's sojourn paid handsome dividends, allowing Winwood and Capaldi the opportunity to develop a remarkable song writing relationship, the strength of which has been overshadowed in rock history by more famous song writing partnerships.

The first two albums, *Mr. Fantasy* (1967) and *Traffic* (1968) are classics of British rock. As well as demonstrating the enormous talents of the band individually, not least the sharp funky drive of Capaldi's drumming, the Winwood-Capaldi writing team was already fully fledged on such numbers as *Pearly Queen, Who Knows What Tomorrow May Bring* and *Forty Thousand Headmen*. The triumverate of great Traffic albums was completed by *John Barleycorn* (1970) and again two of the three best tracks are credited to Winwood-Capaldi, *Empty Pages* and *Freedom Rider*, both wonderful. The last Traffic album was *When The Eagle Flies* (1974), by

which time, Capaldi had already gone to the Muscle Shoals studio to record an excellent solo album, *Oh How We Danced* (1972), featuring master Shoals drummer Roger Hawkins.

On record

Jim Capaldi features on all Traffic albums supplying not just percussion, but vocals, as he does for Paul Kossoff on *Koss* (1977) and Luther Grosvenor's *Under Open Skies* (1971). Of his remaining seven solo albums, *Short Cut Draw Blood* (1975) is probably the best from which came a surprise hit single, a remake of Roy Orbison's *Love Hurts*.

Ed Cassidy

Everything about Ed Cassidy and his position as a drummer is strange. He's over 50 years old, a part-time antiques dealer, bald and original member of a cult sixties band, Spirit, that defied categorisation then and is still resiliantly holding out despite going through more resurrections than Billy Graham.

Ed Cassidy was originally a jazz drummer sideman to such luminaries as Thelonius Monk, Cannonball Adderly and Gerry Mulligan. In the melting pot of the mid Sixties Los Angeles club scene arose a highly respected outfit called the Rising Sons featuring Cassidy, Taj Mahal, Ry Cooder and Jesse Ed Davis. Unfortunately nothing came of this astonishing amalgam although there is apparently an Italian bootleg of studio quality in existence. Cassidy reappeared as the drummer in a band which started out as the Red Roosters, became Spirits Rebellious and then just Spirit in 1967. The line up was Cassidy, Mark Andes (bass), Randy California (guitars), (who may or may not be Cassidy's step-son, depending which article you read), John Locke (keyboards) and Jay Ferguson (vocals).

The first three albums plus *The Twelve Dreams of Dr. Sardonicus* (1970) finished by producer David Briggs after the band split up for the first time, are Spirit's definitive statements – even if Randy California has been quoted as saying that for *Sardonicus* the band wanted to make a concept album but couldn't think of a concept. These albums were eclectic in the extreme and exciting for being so, punctuated by delightful Cassidy jazz fill-ins and mini solos where his long experience came to the fore; some of

his rock drumming on the other hand tended towards the unsubtle and unimaginative.

On these early albums Cassidy displayed a great sense of time and rhythm, carried over to their exhilarating live performances where Cassidy would start a solo on the kit (including that marvellous boomy bass drum on a stand to one side), then leave the kit to play the floor, mike stands, anything in perfect time, before returning to the drums. These interesting variations excited audiences more used to getting a good book and a torch out when drum solos began.

The band went through various revivals in the 1970s and more recently the UK record label Beggars Banquet finally released a remixed version of *Potatoland* (1981) which had been sitting in various record company vaults for years. They released a great single *Turn To The Right* and played sell out concerts in Britain to a whole new audience who were just as ecstatic as they had been in more balmy days.

On record

Ed Cassidy appears on all Spirit albums, the best being *Spirit* (1968), *The Family That Plays Together* (1968), *Clear Spirit* (1969) and *12 Dreams of Dr. Sardonicus* (1970). Not surprisingly, Cassidy played on Randy California's solo effort *Kaptain Copter And The Twirly Birds* (1972).

Clem Cattini

A British drummer who has been on the rock scene for over thirty years since his early days as sometime drummer with Johnny Kidd and The Pirates. Cattini's major flirtation with stardom, however, came with the Tornadoes, originally formed in 1960 as a session group also backing Billy Fury. In 1962, they found themselves with an enormous space-age hit called *Telstar* and followed up with others in a similar vein, putting up a brief challenge to the Shadows as leaders in this particular pop genre. But brief it was, and when it all died away, the band broke up and went their separate ways, Cattini establishing himself on the session circuit, with the Bee Gees in the early Seventies and more recently as a producer.

On record

Apart from the recorded output of the Tornadoes, EPs like *Telstar* (1963) and albums such as *Tornado Rock* (1963), Cattini's session work has included: *With A Little Help From My*

Friends (1969) & *Joe Cocker* (1970), *Lou Reed* (1972), *Stranded* (1971) Edwards Hand with ex-Colosseum guitarist James Litherland and John Wetton, *Mystic Line* Phil Everly (1975), *Hurt* Chris Spedding (1977), *Songwriter* Justin Hayward (1977), *Tarot Suite* Mike Batt (1979).

Ndugu Leon Chancler

Water-tight funky drummer with a big reputation within the 'fusion' scene and reckoned by some critics to be the best drummer Weather Report ever had. Has also done some solo work of late.

On record (Selected)
Feel (1974), *I Love The Blues* (1975), *The Aura Will Prevail* (1975), *Liberated Fantasies* (1976), *From Me To You* (1977) all George Duke, *Inherit The Wind* (1980) Wilton Felder (Crusaders), *Mavardishi* Herbie Hancock (1971), *Mr. Handy* (1980), *Routes* Ramsey Lewis (1980), side one only, *Identify Yourself* O'Jays (1979), *Year 2000* (1980), *Minnie* Minnie Ripperton (1979), *Barboletta* (1974) and *Amigos* (1976 – for Santana of which he was a band member during this time), *Tail Spinnin'* Weather Report (1975).

Michael Clarke

With no professional experience when he first began with the Byrds, Michael Clarke managed to play with just everyone of note in American country rock during the Sixties.

Merely by looking the part, he found himself in the Byrds first line-up in 1964 and was with them through their greatest years of hit singles and albums to 1967 at which point the band collapsed and Clarke went to The Dillard/Clark band with Doug Dillard, Gene Clark and Bernie Leadon (1968-69). From there he moved with Bernie Leadon to the Flying Burrito Brothers, whose line-up included Gram Parsons, 'Sneaky' Pete Kleinow and ex-Byrd Chris Hillman, until 1971 when he dropped out of the music scene altogether. During the Seventies, apart from the odd session, he was included in the line-up of Firefall, an MOR country rock band with ex-Burrito Rick Roberts and former Spirit bassist Mark Andes.

On record
Michael Clarke has contributed to some very fine albums; the early Byrds material needs no introduction, but there are also: *Gene Clark and The Gosdin Brothers* (1967), *Fantastic Expedition – Dillard and Clark* (1968), *Burrito Deluxe – The Flying Burrito Brothers* (1970), *Last of the Red Hot Burritos* (1971), *Roger McGuinn* (1973), *Firefall* (1976), *Luna Sea* Firefall (1977), *Elan* (1978).

Doug Clifford

Based on his work in Creedence Clearwater Revival, Doug Clifford can be regarded as one of the finest white drummers playing 50's-oriented rock'n'roll and with bassist Stu Cook, formed an unrivalled rhythm section playing this kind of music. CCR went through two earlier metamorphoses, first as a high school group called Tommy Fogerty and the Blue Velvets and then (reluctantly) as the Golliwogs, the name change being a proviso of Fantasy Record's recording contract.

Under this moniker, success was still proving elusive, but they plugged on, gambled on turning professional in 1967 with the name Creedence Clearwater Revival and then it all began to happen. For the next four years, inspired by the genius of John Fogerty and driven on by that pulsating rhythm section, their records weren't cast in black plastic, but in metal – virtually everything they did went gold or platinum and they played everywhere to packed houses. When the band finally split up in 1972, Clifford and Cook carried on as a session team and took their talents most notably to the Don Harrison Band. Doug Clifford was in the Steve Miller Band that played Knebworth in 1975.

On record
THE CCR albums (which were really put together deliberately as collections of singles), were *Bayou Country* (1969), *Green River* (1969) and *Willie and The Poor Boys* (1970) containing such classic material as *Proud Mary, Bad Moon Rising, Born on the Bayou* and *Lodi.* Listen to that rhythm and weep.

The clean, sharp Clifford-Cook sound can also be heard on two good Don Harrison band albums, *The Don Harrison Band* (1976) and *Red Hot* (1976), particularly the latter one.

Billy Cobham

Ask the ordinary 'rock fan in the street' who he reckons is the world's best drummer and the chances are that the name of Billy Cobham will be

uttered in the first breath. Whether Cobham *is* the best, is another matter, depending on what you mean by best and in what musical context, but theology aside, Cobham is one of the visible greats, as the drummer who has done more to make people aware of drumming by his dazzling skills, than anyone since Buddy Rich. Unlike other instrumental maestros, however, he has not spawned a bevy of imitators (how many drummers have you heard that play and sound like Billy Cobham?), but by his thoughtful,

Billy Cobham

progressive approach to percussion, he ushered in the age of the intelligent drummer and in the process, gave direction and impetus to a whole new style of drumming which influenced thousands of young drummers. The dominant force in fusion drumming, he brought together the tonal colours of jazz and the power of rock in a unique synthesis, utilising a combination of Tony Williams-inspired single stroke rolls and fast bass drum/snare/cymbal inter-play and the innovation of dampened-down tom toms with little or no "ring", which allowed every stroke to be heard as he tumbled round the kit.

He has also been an innovatory user of much new drum technology over the years, including North drums and the 'Chinese' style cymbal with the edges turned up, producing a harsh sound which penetrates effectively through amplified instrumentation. Now a Tama drummer, he has sported a triple bass Sunburst kit with a triple snare drum combo mounted on one stand. Cobham does many Tama clinics, demonstrating the hardware that he largely helped to design.

Born in Panama in 1944, and playing self taught from the age of 8, Cobham had a distinguished jazz career in the Sixties with Horace Silver, the Billy Taylor Trio, Stanley Turrentine, Kenny Burrell, the New York Jazz Sextet and Grosvenor Washington. He was also in an early fusion outfit in the late Sixties called Dreams, with the Brecker Brothers. And then came the incomparable Mahavishnu Orchestra – John McLaughlin, Jan Hammer, Rick Laird, Jerry Goodman and William Cobham, playing supersonic jazz/rock. When they came to Britain, it was the first time most fans had ever seen Billy Cobham. Nobody had ever seen such whirlwind, power drumming that was so absolutely controlled; his lightning snare drum work at very low volume was phenomenal. Few, if any, drummers even played the same way – he abandoned the time honoured, institutionalised left hand snare/right hand hi-hat pattern.

As Lenny White had realised before, if your right hand is the stronger, why should it be relegated to doing the least work.

It was a tragedy that a band of such influence should have broken up in such acrimony and it was particularly distressing for Billy Cobham. He fell in with a poor management who didn't know how to promote a non-vocal act. He toured with George Duke in 1974 and then with his own band. The audiences cheered when the drum kit was rolled on, but it wasn't enough. Probably a better band drummer than leader, he suc-cumbed to the pressure of the record company for "output" because of heavy financial commitments and was forced into producing bland funky nonsense. Even then it didn't sell. It was not easy for him to please either himself, his fans or his creditors and at one time he was so disillusioned with music that he wouldn't even have a record player in the house. Therefore, 1979 was a time for rejoicing when he did a series of reunion concerts with McLaughlin, Jack Bruce and keyboardist Stu Goldberg. Since Mahavishnu days, the only real recording bright spots were his first two solo albums *Spectrum* (1973) and *Crosswinds* (1974). Spectrum also show-cased the then unknown guitar ace, Tommy Bolin. With his extraordinary skill at leading off patterns to the left and the right, keeping the whole rhythmic flow in constant motion, the sight and sound of Billy Cobham in full flight is unmatched in drumming.

On record
Inner Mounting Flame (1971), *Birds of Fire* (1973) Mahavishnu Orchestra, *Love, Devotion and Surrender* McLaughlin and Carlos Santana (1973 – particularly *A Love Supreme*), *Spectrum* Billy Cobham (1973 – particularly *Quadrant 4*, the breathtaking opening track. Whole record shops stood still when this first came over the speakers.) *Crosswinds* Billy Cobham (1974).

Phil Collins

One of Britain's most consistent, versatile and popular musicians, the hyperactive Phil Collins has excelled as a drummer, singer, producer and songwriter.

A highly inventive and schooled drummer in the Bruford mould, Collins demonstrated his characteristic strength of will and determination at an early age, by selling his train set to buy a drum kit – no mean sacrifice for a wee lad. As a child actor, his greatest triumph was as the artful Dodger in the West End production of *Oliver*, before playing in numerous bands including the much-touted Flaming Youth. Joining Genesis in 1970 after answering an advert, he was the fourth drummer, following on from John Mayhew, Chris Stewart and John Silver, who all eventually left the business. It took *Foxtrot* (1972) and the UK tour of that year to put Genesis on the map. With a unique brand of orchestrated symphonic rock music variously labelled "art-rock" or "pomp rock", the band was driven by Collins' rifle-shot snare drum and rolling tom-toms, an English interpretation of an American style of drumming. They embarked on punishing tour schedules but grew in stature and confidence all the time. Then in 1975, came the shock departure of their creative genius, Peter Gabriel and everyone thought that was it. But Phil Collins astounded them all; calling upon all his past theatrical experience, he hopped off the drum stool, up to the front of the stage, let rip with his own highly distinctive plaintive vocal sound and led Genesis to even greater glories and even longer tours. On the road, drumming duties were shared with Bill Bruford and then ex-Zappa, ex-Weather Report drummer, Chester Thompson.

But, as if grabbing the reins of a top flight band wasn't enough, in the same year as Gabriel's departure, Collins assembled Brand X for occasional gigs with Percy Jones (bass), Robin Lumley (keyboards) and John Goodsall (guitar). Although his appearances with the band grew fewer as his commitments increased, Phil Collins seemed to enjoy his outings with this dynamic fusion-style ensemble immensely and his drumming took on a more exploratory and aggressive feel. With this band, he could concentrate on just playing drums (usually Premier) and he was very much at home.

It was in 1981, however, that Phil Collins put the icing on the cake of a highly successful career, with the release of his solo album *Face Value*, one of the best albums of the year. A gorgeously rich amalgam of styles, brimming with good qualities, not least the now famous 'open-spaced' live drum sound used to such startling and dramatic effect on *In The Air Tonight* and also on Peter Gabriel's 1980 album on which Collins also plays. Taking into account the totality of Collins' involvement with this album, from writing to production, *Face Value* must stand as his highest achievement to date.

In an attempt to ease out the wizened has-beens of Yesteryear (i.e. the musicians) from their precious poll, a famous weekly rock paper that ought to know better, did away with separate categories of instrument and just had one – "instrumentalist". Phil Collins won it.

On record
As well as recording with Genesis and Brand X, Phil Collins has been a

frequent visitor to the studio as a session musician. Indeed, apart from *Trick Of The Tail* (1976) and individual tracks from *Foxtrot* (1972) like *Supper's Ready* and the awesome *Apocalypse in ⅜*, Collins' most interesting drum work has been outside of the context of Genesis. His best work includes *Unorthodox Behaviour* (1976) and *Moroccan Roll* (1977), both Brand X; subtle, delicate and lyrical drumming on *Grace and Danger* (1980) by John Martyn, hard edged on *Peter Gabriel* (1980), and fluid on Jack Lancaster's neglected gem *Marscape* (1976).

The many facets of a talented musician.

Bobby Colomby

Important as the only surviving member of the original Blood, Sweat and Tears that he formed with Al Kooper and Steve Katz back in 1967. It seems that the band's initial motivations were slightly suspect – polished up rock music with a highly technical big band jazz veneer and so perhaps fans should not have felt quite so betrayed when they moved into the easy listening market where, incidentally, they have done exceptionally well saleswise, as have Chicago in a similar vein. Both bands promised much, but finished up producing aural wallpaper. Colomby has now moved into record production.

On record
The first album *Child Is Father To The Man* (1968) is probably the best, but *Greatest Hits* (1972) is a good summary of their work. If you can listen past David Clayton Thomas' grating over-the-top vocals, you will discover some neatly defined jazz percussion, Colomby always an interesting drummer.

Gerry Conway

The names of the top American session rock drummers are well known to music fans everywhere – Steve Gadd, Jeff Porcaro, Russ Kunkel and Jim Keltner, to name but four. But Britain too, has some very prolific session drummers with long and impressive track records, one being Gerry Conway. In the early to mid Seventies, he operated largely in the incestuous arena of British folk/rock artists on the Island roster but has spread his wings a bit of late.

He started out as band drummer in a pioneering folk ensemble called Eclection who just preceded Fairport Convention onto the scene in mid-1967 with some interesting, but problematical music from a marketing point of view. Despite critical acclaim, they failed to make sufficient impact and folded around the end of 1969. Conway teamed up with the much-missed Sandy Denny in Fotheringay after she had split from Fairport but the band was sadly short-lived and she embarked on a solo career using Conway, Richard Thompson and Tull bassist to-be, Dave Pegg, in her backing band during 1971. Apart from a mountain of session work, Conway has toured with Cat Stevens and Chris Farlowe.

On record
Eclection (1968), *Matthews Southern Comfort* (1970) & *If You Saw Through My Eyes* all by Matthews Southern Comfort (1971), *Fotheringay* (1970), *Northstar Grass Man And The Ravens* (1971) & *Like An Old Fashioned Waltz* (1973) all by Sandy Denny, *Rock On The Bunch* (1972 – ad hoc association of friends including Sandy Denny, Richard Thompson, Trevor Lucas and Ashley Hutchings. They recorded one album.), *Rosie* (1973), *Tour Sampler* (1973), *Chronicles* (1976) – all by Fairport Convention (The ins and outs of this group were hideously complicated – ask Pete Frame!; Conway was never a band member, but played at least these sessions.) *Whatever's For Us* Joan Armatrading (1974), *Slow Dazzle* John Cale (1975), *Short Cut Draw Blood* Jim Capaldi (1975), *Down at Rachel's Place* Mike d'Abo (1972), *Loving and Free* Kiki Dee (1973), *Live* Chris Farlowe (1975), *Rocking Duck* Grimms (1973), *How Sweet To Be An Idiot* Neil Innes (1973), *Fresh Liver* (1973), *Sold Out* Scaffold (1975 – All part of the Neil Innes, Roger McGough, John Gorman, Mike McGear, Andy Roberts 'a laugh, a song and a poem' experiments. Bonzo Dog meets the Liverpool Scene.) *October* Claire Hammill (1973), *Summer Solstice* Tim Hart and Maddy Prior (1972), *Smiling Men With Bad Reputations* Mike Heron (1971), *Liquid Acrobats* Incredible String Band (1971), *Hiding* Albert Lee (1979), (Conway and Lee both played in the Chris Farlowe band of 1975.) *Lark* (1972) & *Not A Little Girl Anymore* Linda Lewis (1975), *Easy* Ralph McTell (1973), *Teaser and the Firecat* (1971), *Catch Bull At Four* (1972), *Foreigner* (1973), *Buddah and the Chocolate Box* (1974) & *Number* (1975) all by Cat Stevens, *Zero She*

Flies (1970) & *Modern Times* (1975) by Al Stewart, *Broadsword* Jethro Tull (1982).

Few British session drummers appear on American albums, but John Hiatt used Gerry Conway on *Slugline* (1979).

Ray Cooper

It is a rare happening when a session drummer comes out of the shadows into the public eye; when it happens to a session percussionist, it's about the music business equivalent of The Second Coming. Such a phenomenon is Ray Cooper. As a master of acoustic and tuned percussion, he goes back to John Dankworth and Cleo Laine, Maynard Ferguson, TV shows like Simon Dee (remember?) and the orchestra pits of countless theatres. At one time he was doing so many sessions a week, he wasn't always sure who he was playing for. His credentials in the rock world include playing for the likes of Joan Armatrading, Nilsson, Rod Stewart, the Rolling Stones, Rick Wakeman, Carly Simon, Brian Ferry and David Essex but he is probably best known for his association with Elton John.

When Pinner's finest decided to ditch his backing musicians and tour with just one other, he chose Ray Cooper. The gigs were a sensation with Cooper a blur of energy in a three piece suit (ironic that such apparel should be regarded as bizarre – which it was – when his early jazz work probably demanded it).

Cooper handles the full range of percussion including drums, congas, marimbas, xylophone, bells, gong, kettle drums, cowbell and more esoteric items like windchimes, shaker vibes and jawbones. And he uses them in a thoroughly artistic and schooled fashion – they are by no means mere sound fillers. The tambourine, for example, can be something the lead singer whacks during the encore numbers to keep his hands busy or it can be subtly introduced, adding tonal colours and variety, often to devastating effect. There is a right time and a right way to play all these instruments, even the humble triangle.

On record
Bands like Santana and The Art Ensemble of Chicago place high value on the use of all kinds of weird and wonderful percussion and are well versed in their potentialities. Listen to Ray Cooper, particularly on Elton John albums like *Captain Fantastic*

(1974) and *Rock of The Westies* (1975) as the superb production allows what would often get lost in muddy mixing and atrocious recording quality to come shining through with literally bell-like clarity.

Stewart Copeland

American born Copeland is a vital ingredient in one of the most phenomenally successful bands of recent years – the Police. After a brief spell with Curved Air, during which time

Left: Stewart Copeland
Below: John Coughlan

he appeared on two albums *Midnight Wire* (1975) and *Airborne* (1976), he approached Sting with the idea of an updated Cream/Hendrix trio but with a simpler music style.

The razzle dazzle surrounding the band in general and Sting in particular, has tended to obscure their fine musicianship and the key to this simpler style has been the ingenious utilisation of diamond hard reggae rhythms in a pulsating rock context played sharp and punchy with three beats instead of two and no backbeat. In this unique way you have a white drummer playing reggae but with twists, which I would suggest is very effective despite the criticism that the band has faced for playing what has been dubbed (no pun intended)

'ersatz reggae', harking back to the interminably boring 'can the white man sing the blues' arguments of fifteen years ago. Copeland has also been innovative in comparatively early use of Tama drums, now a world leader in the drum market. He still plays Tama but has also become fascinated with drum electronics while continuing to play an acoustic set up with Tama Octobans; 'gadgets' include a Roland chorus echo unit and drum synthesizer integrated into the overall sound. One of the more exciting and interesting drummers to have emerged of late from the upheavals of the British music scene.

On record
Regatta de Blanc (1979 – particularly the title track and the great echo rim

shots on *Walkin' On The Moon*), *Outlandos D'Amour* (1978 – particularly *So Lonely*).

John Coughlan

Status Quo's ever present drummer until recently. The band started life as the Spectres (or Spectors) and as Status Quo had two hit singles in 1968, *Pictures of Matchstick Men* and *Ice In The Sun*. It was downhill all the way after that, until they discovered those magic chords and denims and they haven't looked back since. In that time, Coughlan drove the band from behind his Premier kit, honing down 4/4 rock beats to their most simplistic as riff laden hits followed one after the other. Effective, with no frills but with no thrills either. Coughlan began occasional outings with his own band Diesel, deciding this year to give it all his attention and so after 15 years, he quit Status Quo. His replacement was former Original Mirrors and Honeybus (!) drummer, Pete Kircher. More of the same? I suppose so.

On record
Blue For You (1976) will suffice as an example of what Status Quo is all about. And when all said and done, there are a helluva lot of punters who like it.

Richard Coughlan

In the town of Canterbury during the mid Sixties, there was a band called Wilde Flowers which between '63 and '67 contained founder members of Soft Machine, Gong, National Health, Kevin Ayers and the Whole World, Hatfield and the North and Caravan. Into Wilde Flowers during 1965 came an ex-dental technician, Richard Coughlan, former drummer in such unlikely ensembles as the Stourside Stompers, a trad jazz band; Les Paynes Dance Band, Chaos and the Earl Gutheridge Explosion, which could *only* have been a Sixties band.

During its four year history, Wilde Flowers lost Robert Wyatt and Hugh Hopper (Soft Machine), Daevid Allen (Gong) and Kevin Ayers eventually leaving Pye Hastings, David Sinclair and Richard Coughlan to form Caravan. Hastings and Coughlan remained ever-present members, David and Richard Sinclair between them, moving in and out of music, going solo and playing with Hatfield

and the North. Only in 1982, has the original line-up got back together again to record. Caravan have always been an enigmatic band, quintessentially British, ploughing a relatively lonely furrow of orchestrated quasi-avant garde jazz rock that actually worked – much softer and less demanding than Soft Machine, while managing to avoid the often overblown dramatics of Yes and Genesis. They have retained a loyal band of supporters in England and on the Continent, even garnering some American success with *Cunning Stunts* (1975).

Yet, for this author, at any rate, they are frustrating, because in Richard Coughlan they had through the years, a drummer who could really drive this band along with spirit, invention and a distinctive funky style virtually unique in this brand of British rock. On the other hand his drumming has been, on occasion, dull and predictable, holding the beat down, throwing in a few repetitive fill-ins and not stretching out as the music demanded, the effect of which was to hold the music back in a sense.

Coughlan appears on all Caravan albums and they are all worth listening to musically, if not necessarily lyrically, retaining an admirable freshness and durability. Two contrasting examples of Coughlan's drumming will, I hope, suffice to illustrate my point – the too-linear stodginess and lack of tension in *Nine Feet Underground* from *In The Land of Grey And Pink* (1971) and the brightness of *The Love In Your Eye* and the rest of that twelve minute track on *Waterloo Lily* (1972). The contrasts are most marked on Caravan's longer pieces where the chance exists for something to happen – or not.

Terry Cox

An experienced jazz-oriented drummer who, with his bass partner Danny Thompson, served time in Alexis Korner's Blues Incorporated before moving their combined talents to Pentangle in 1967. Pentangle were a successful amalgam of the influences and experiences of the individual members, Cox and Thompson supplying the jazz and blues elements – Jansch, Renbourne and Jacqui McShee, the folk inspiration. All these modes were important to the initial success of this band – Cox and Thompson were no mere sidemen and the first album *The Pentangle* (1968) demonstrated

the extent to which musical boundaries could be effectively breached, given the right chemistry. It was the correct mix that was important so that the band became rather less interesting when the folk side began to take over, particularly in the use of 16th century style percussion on *Basket of Light* (1969). Eventually, Cox and Thompson were reduced to a secondary role until 1972 when the group split. Now, after ten years, Terry Cox has rejoined with Bert Jansch as the guitarist-cum-music shop owner takes to the road once more.

On record
Cox's amount of session work seemed to increase as his interest in Pentangle declined and he can be heard on: *Space Oddity* David Bowie (1969), *Open The Door* The Humblebums (1970 – with Billy Connolly and Gerry Rafferty), *Elton John* (1970) & *Madman Across The Water* (1970) by Elton John, *Say No More* Linda Lewis (1971), *Changes* John Williams (1971 – Sky).

He also appeared on the Sallyangie album *Children of the Sun* (1968) featuring Sally Oldfield and brother Mike, before he decided to do it all himself. Later Cox sessions include Mike Batt's *Tarot Suite* (1979).

Peter Criss

Peter Criss was, until recently, the drummer with the Cat persona from Kiss, the staggeringly successful heavy metal band more merchandised than any other band in the world, with a battery of gold and platinum records to their credit.

Based on albums like *Destroyer* produced by Bob Ezrin (who produced *The Wall* for Pink Floyd), Kiss are a much more technically accomplished band than their gonzo reputation would suggest. In Criss, for example, they had not a mindless tub thumper, but a thoughtful jazz-influenced drummer who copped lessons from Gene Krupa no less and brought aspects of the master's solo work into his own. In addition, he is a successful song writer whose own material was out of line with Kiss' requirements, prompting his departure. *Beth*, taken from *Destroyer* (1976) went double gold as a single, even though the other members of the band didn't want to include it originally. He is now spreading his musical wings much further and learning more about jazz

Peter Criss

rhythms, in the process reducing the size of his Pearl/Zildjian kit by about half. Criss was taken into Kiss when they answered his anguished advert in Rolling Stone 'drummer willing to do *anything*' – now he can.

On record

Criss is on all Kiss albums, the best being a sophisticated concept album *Destroyer* (1976) and also *Alive* (1977). Most of the rest are very hard on the ears, mainly due to horrendous production and substandard material.

John Cuffley

Member of the Climax Blues Band since 1973 when he replaced George Newsome, the band's original drummer since formation as the Climax Chicago Blues Band in 1968. The band has largely kept to its jazzy blues/rock formula through the years, becoming more popular in America than in Britain, where they were largely forgotten, (similarly with Fleetwood Mac and Savoy Brown/Foghat).

Cuffley is a busy muscular drummer with an excellent American-style swing feel, a good sense of dynamics and able to cope fluidly with several styles within one number such as *Flight* on the *FM/LIVE* album (1974). Cuffley features on all Climax albums from *Rich Man* (1972) onwards.

Cliff Davies

Drummer, lyricist and vocalist, who moved from the Roy Young Band in 1974 to join If, replacing Dennis Elliott, now of Foreigner. If were a much admired jazz-rock outfit, who never achieved the success they deserved. Davies joined a reshuffled line-up which included Dick Morris-

sey, one of the founder members and Geoff Whitehorn, a brilliant but ludicrously underrated guitarist and overall the band now had a harder edge. However, success still eluded them and they finally broke up in 1975. The album they released that year, *Tea Breaks Over, Back On Your Heads* was a Next City production, the same company involved in the launching of Ted Nugent on his solo career with his first album in 1976. It was to the Ted Nugent band Cliff Davies moved, featuring on subsequent Nugent albums, contributing some meaty drumming while managing (somehow) to avoid being ponderous – deserving of some sort of award one would imagine, given Nugent's sledgehammer material and his unique ear-piercing service – both ears at once.

On record

The Roy Young Band (1971) & *Mr. Funky* (1972) by Roy Young, *Not Just A Bunch Of Pretty Faces* (1974) & *Tea Breaks Over, Back On Your Heads* (1978) by If, (much of the If material on these albums was Davies-penned.), *Ted Nugent* (1976), *Free For All* (1976), (particularly *Turn It Up*), *Cat Scratch Fever* (1977), *Double Live Gonzo* (1978) all by Ted Nugent.

Brian 'Blinky' Davison

As a member of The Nice, Blinky Davison was one of the truly great drummers to have emerged from the British 'underground' scene during the Sixties. The start was relatively inauspicious – drummer in P. P. Arnold's soul band with the rest of what was to become the Nice – Keith Emerson, Lee Jackson (bass) and David O'List (guitar) who left after the release of the band's first album *Thoughts of Emerlist DavJack* (1967). The stage was left to Keith Emerson, whose flamboyant stage act carried over and developed in Emerson, Lake and Palmer. But despite being overshadowed by Emerson, Davison was just as good a musician on his instrument (and possibly better). To watch him flowing round his tiny Hayman kit with breathtaking dexterity was sheer delight (the first drummer I ever saw do a one-handed snare roll) – a superb technician without being in the least cold or unemotional.

After the Nice came to an end (the split *not* being amicable), Davison tried his hand as a band leader with

Every Which Way – it didn't work. Neither did the Davison/Jackson attempt to recreate the Nice as Refugee in 1974 with Patrick Moraz as Keith Emerson. When Yes called, the offer for Moraz was too tempting and the band fell apart. They produced one album with some fine playing on it so the collapse of the band came as a bitter blow to both Jackson and Davison.

Apart from a brief spell with Gong, Blinky Davison tragically dropped out of the music scene altogether although rumour has it that he's playing around the Notting Hill area of West London these days. Ironic, when one hears the justified accolades heaped on drummers like Phil Collins and Bill Bruford – Brian Davison deserves to be considered in the same league.

On record

Thoughts of Emerlist DavJack (1967), *Ars Longa Vita Brevis* (1968), *The Nice* (1969 – particularly the incomparable *Rondo*), *Five Bridges Suite* Emerson, Lake & Palmer (1970), *Elergy* (1971 – plus numerous repackagings), *Every Which Way* (1970), *Flat Baroque and Berserk* Roy Harper (1970), *Refugee* (1974).

John Densmore

John Densmore – drummer with the Doors. Their power as a collective unit was formidable, Densmore's thick sound creating the necessary solidity for Kreiger and Manzarek's eerie swirling melody lines to play around the lyrics, in their own way re-interpreting, as well as supporting Morrison's, stark visions of death and alienation.

The suffocation and the tension of the music seemed so unforced – it was a musical black hole drawing the listener inexorably in with celebratory crescendos and sinister bass rhythms. A unique chemistry that was impossible to maintain once Morrison had gone, although *Other Voices* (1971), was a reasonable effort. The other post Morrison album, *Full Circle* (1972) was, however, a dog.

After disagreements with Manzarek, Densmore and Krieger formed the Butts Band with guitarist Jess Roden and keyboardist Phil Chen. Two albums followed, one with this line-up, the other featuring new musicians. Both efforts were dismal and they called it a day around 1975. Since then, John Densmore has appeared on a Robby Krieger solo album of

1977.

It is often the way that when musicians have had such a career experience, there is nowhere else to go and anything different invariably has to be an anti-climax and there is an element of "burn-out" as well. Back in the Sixties, Joan Didion wrote a piece called *Waiting For Morrison* – perhaps they still are.

On record

Particular tracks: *Break On Through, My Eyes Have Seen You, When The Music's Over, The End, Light My Fire, Waiting For The Sun, Soul Kitchen.*

Barry De Souza

British session drummer whose varied recordings have included: *Transformer* Lou Reed (1972), *A Tear And A Smile* (1972), *Strong In The Sun* (1973 – by Tir Na Nog – an Irish folk duo who achieved brief fame then disappeared), *Modern Times* Al Stewart (1975), *Something In My Life* Tom Paxton (1975), *Far Beyond These Castle Walls* (1975), *Spanish Train* (1975) by Chris de Burgh, *The Kick Inside* Kate Bush (1978), *Baby Faced Killer* David Byron (1978), *Gomm With The Wind* Ian Gomm (1978 – ex-Brinsley Schwartz), *The Dukes* (1979 – a much touted band with Miller Anderson, Jimmy McCulloch, Ronnie Leahy and Charlie Tumahai which folded almost immediately when McCulloch died), *Matthew Fisher* (1980).

Liberty De Vitto

Billy Joel's ever-present, classy studio and touring drummer. Being a "percussive" strident keyboard player, Joel and De Vitto have a tremendous empathy on stage, feeding off one another as the drummer snaps in a snare or hi-hat accent to add extra bite to Joel lyrics on such songs of *The Stranger* or *Big Shot*.

There is much to admire in De Vitto's drumming, (quite apart from the vibrant sound of the drums and cymbals themselves), small things often but devastating nonetheless – the choked hi-hat opener to *The Stranger*, and the tom-tom triplet that punctuates the song throughout or the hi-hat/snare patterns of *Zanzibar*, taking off into a rippling jazz rhythm and back into the main funky theme. De Vitto is a great artist on cymbals, using tom-toms relatively sparingly but always right where you feel they

ought to come. A pleasure to listen to.

On record

Some of his best work comes on *The Stranger* (1977) and *52nd Street* (1978).

Ritchie Dharma

Not exactly a household name but a drummer of no mean talent. Impressive both live *and* on record with the Mick Abrahams band of the early Seventies (notably his dexterous bass drum patterns) and it is surprising, listening to his playing, that the name of Ritchie Dharma has not featured more prominently on rock album credit listings over the years.

On record

Mick Abrahams (1971) & *At Last* (1972) by Mick Abrahams, *Window* Michael Chapman (1971), *Transformer* Lou Reed (1972), *Play Don't Worry* Mick Ronson (1975), *First Starring Role* Bob Sargeant (1975).

Brian Downey

Brian Downey and Phil Lynott were school mates in Dublin and first played together in a band called the Black Eagles – Lynott was the vocalist while Downey's audition was to go away for two weeks and learn *You Really Got Me*. He got the job. Some sources say that the two friends played together in a blues band called Sugar Shack, others say that only Downey was a member. At any rate, they came together in Orphanage later on and from this came the first line-up of Thin Lizzy in 1970 with Eric Bell on guitar and the success of their first single *Whiskey In The Jar* a top ten hit in November 1972.

But there were problems ahead, primarily because they couldn't find a guitarist after Eric Bell left. Before the arrival of Scott Gorham and Brian Robertson in 1974, Lynott and Downey almost called it a day. However, the big break came, appropriately enough with the release of *Jailbreak* in 1976. Brian Downey has been ever present in the band apart from Lizzy's autumn tour of 1978 when ex-Gillan drummer Mark Nauseef deputised.

Downey has always been the quiet member of the band, leaving the Brian Robertsons of this world to play the personality game (until one day Robertson overplayed his hand and almost lost it in an internal "difference of opinion"). However, there is nothing laid back about Downey's

thunderous (but never excessive) drum style, although this is not to imply that Lizzy can be lumped in with the run-of-the-mill British heavy rock juggernauts – they've got too much class for that.

On record

Jailbreak (1976) is still the best album; worth noting is *Emerald* for the way that Downey translates traditional Irish folk percussion rhythms into the rock context of Lizzy's Celtic War anthem.

Drum Kits

In many respects, the acoustic rock drum kit has changed little since the war, and all its individual elements were around in one form or another for many years previous.

Essentially, the basic kit consists of a bass drum (about 22 inches in diameter) struck by a foot pedal; a top tom-tom (13×9) mounted on the bass drum; a free-standing floor tom-tom on the right, and centrally positioned on its own stand, a metal shelled snare drum (6½×14). The other drums are usually wood-shelled, ranging between 5 and 12 ply, maple being the preferred wood. To the left of the snare is the hi-hat, comprising two cymbals which are clashed together using a foot pedal, and two cymbals on either side of the bass drum, (or one might be mounted on the bass drum itself), a 'ride' for timekeeping and a crash for accents. Ringo Starr was using a set-up like this in the mid-sixties and the unfussy kits of many contemporary new wave drummers underline a continuity in simplistic hardware on a different level, technically, financially and philosophically, from the large kits of their heavy rock and fusion counterparts.

The modern drum kit evolved from the clubs of New Orleans and the South, where, originally banned from having drums as slaves in case they were used to signal rebellion, black musicians took the hardware of white military rudimental drumming, the snare and the bass, put them on the floor and combined standard marching rudiments with African tribal rhythms to produce the patterns of jazz. Already by 1908 the world famous Ludwig Drum Company had developed a pedal for the bass drum. The hi-hat has literally grown up over the years. Originally, it stood only a few inches off the floor, making its appearance in the twenties as the 'low-hat' in America and the 'sock-cymbal' in Europe. The demand to play the 'low-hat' with sticks rather than be limited to foot-controlled off beats only, led to the raising of the 'low-hat' to higher levels.

Although vastly more sophisticated in design and technology, the manifold percussive paraphernalia of drummers like Neil Peart of Rush and the Chinese cymbals used widely since their adoption by Billy Cobham all have their antecedents in days gone by. Thick, squat Chinese cymbals were used originally by Dixieland drummers until the demand for cymbals suitable for playing accent notes rather than for mere novelty, was met by the Turkish company Zildjian who began production of high quality cymbals in America in the twenties. Around the same time, too, drummers had surrounded themselves with a plethora of gimmicks and gadgets – one possible derivation of the word 'traps' is that the tangle of hardware constituted a trap over which the unwary fell in the dark.

However, as drums became more integrated into the overall sounds of popular music in the twenties and thirties, so out went the gimmicks and the kit became much simpler. This further led to the development of jazz drumming as a fine art, so that by the time rock came along, jazz percussion was in the ascendent, executed with infinite skill and virtuosity by such stars as Max Roach, Art Blakey, Buddy Rich and Jo Jones. Rock and R&B drummers were regarded as inadequate upstarts and they lived in the scornful shadow of jazz for many years. Only when rock had demonstrated its colossal impact on music and produced its own star drummers like Jerry Allison and Sandy Nelson, did rock drumming begin to accrue any sort of credibility. But it was still early days; rock drumming did not really come of age until its own parameters had been staked out by the likes of Ginger Baker, Ringo Starr, Keith Moon and John Bonham.

The main companies are Ludwig, Gretsch, Slingerland, and Rogers (American), Sonor (Germany), Premier (England) and the Japanese firms of Pearl, Yamaha and Tama. Until recently, Ludwig were easily the market leaders: all the top drummers swore by them and before import controls were lifted in the Sixties, the much coveted Ludwig drums were smuggled into Britain under all sorts of obscure labels. Then, almost inevitably, the Japanese entered the mar-

ket and patiently built up their expertise over the years with Western help, to the point where Tama, in particular, have captured a significant part of the top end of the professional market, boasting such endorsers as Billy Cobham and Simon Phillips. To their credit, however, Ludwig have not stood still; they are still regarded by many as the Rolls Royce of drums and a significant number of famous drummers have remained loyal to the company with new disciples joining all the time.

Avedis and K. Zildjian ruled the cymbal market for forty years until the early Sixties when their only serious rival appeared in the shape of the Swiss company, Paiste. The last ten years has seen a fierce rivalry develop between the two companies to produce heavy duty cymbals for the rock market and both now sell a wide range through all dimensions and tonal colours, each a tribute to the extremely delicate and subtle technology of cymbal construction. A cymbal sound is born in the special metal alloys when they are still shapeless lumps. From ingot to finished product, a Zildjian cymbal takes five days.

Before the mid-Sixties, the main technological breakthrough was the plastic head which appeared courtesy of Remo in 1957. Calf skins had always been problematical, prone as they were to the vagaries of temperature and humidity. Too warm and they went slack and out of tune – too cold and they could dry out and break, not to mention the thoughtful club patrons who would knock beer all over the drums. Plastic heads were ideal for rock, allowing the drums to cut through the amplified sounds. Since then, Remo have developed 'spot' heads, with an extra layer of plastic in the centre to deaden the sound for studio work and heads that stay in tune even when they are removed from the shell.

Bass drum pedals were also improved, faster and more rugged – the Ludwig Speed King being the most important progression towards the modern pedal. Companies have also produced pedals giving two beats for every strike and twin-beaters for use with single bass drums.

Over the past fifteen years, the main developments have been in relation to size – the phenomenon of the large kit, initiated by Ginger Baker and Keith Moon who doubled up on the drums in the basic kit, and the increase in size of the individual

drums – John Bonham was one of the first to go for the bigger drum sizes like the 26inch bass drum for volume and projection while still playing the basic kit.

Nowadays drummers are able to tune drums to specific notes by using single-headed concert tom toms in groups of eight each with its own note, (or two heads for a brighter sound), or the Remo roto-tom, a shell-less variable pitch tom tom. Boom stands for cymbals make them easier to reach and in general, stands and fittings are now more durable and flexible – Rogers pioneered the Memorilok system allowing for stands to be set into position, so that the drums are at the correct angles right the way through a tour.

Rock drummers have become increasingly involved in the design and promotion of new hardware e.g. Billy Cobham has worked closely with Tama taking the hardware he helped to evolve out for demonstration in drum clinics all over the world. Carl Palmer advised in the construction of the Arbiter auto-tune kit of the mid seventies – the first mass produced kit that dispensed with conventional head adjustment, relying instead on the principle of the screw-top jar for tuning.

The revised interest in dance music and African rhythms has brought the acoustic kit to the fore – recent UK chart singles have featured drums prominently. But the major sound of dance since the late Seventies has been the synthesized sounds of electronic drums. Syndrums became synonymous with disco – the famous 'pew pew' sound tediously repeated on song after song. But they are only one small sector of an expanding and sophisticated technological market, which, however, had never really matched the sound of an acoustic kit. That has changed with the arrival of the British designed Simmons SDS V – six 2inch thick perspex, touch sensitive playing surfaces mounted on stands, including a bass drum pad, capable of producing studio sounds on stage and cutting through the front-line instrumentation with no difficulty. The drummer sits behind it and can either play it like an ordinary kit or programme beats through a computer. During the 1982 Ry Cooder tour of the UK, Jim Keltner used a Simmons in conjunction with conventional hardware. After a gig, the SDS V packs down into a couple of suitcases. It represents a major innovation in percussion.

The drum machines that produce perfect beats that go on for ever at the flick of a switch have caused great controversy – the musicians' unions on both sides of the Atlantic have been concerned over their use in the studio, considering them a threat to their members' livelihoods. Some drummers agree and view them with trepidation, others see them as liberation, most see them as another piece of hardware to add to the armoury of available effects. But even with the improvements that are bound to be made to the Simmons kit and the imitators that will follow, it is unlikely that the acoustic kit will ever be totally superseded – both technologies will coexist and continue to develop side by side.

In the business world at least, the rock drummer is now a much feted individual, particularly those endorsing Japanese products. Tales have been heard of the band who arrive jet-lagged at Tokyo airport – the drum representative is waiting. He approaches the drummer and whisks him off to the hotel in a limo while the lead singer, the star of the show, is left looking at the luggage.

Spencer Dryden

Before joining Jefferson Airplane in October 1966 on the recommendation of ace drummer Earl Palmer, Spencer Dryden had been playing on the jazz circuit with such notables as Charlie Haden and Charles Lloyd. He moved into the San Francisco rock scene with a band called the Ashes (who later had a brief dalliance with fame as the Peanut Butter Conspiracy) until the departure of Skip Spence from Airplane to form Moby Grape created the vacancy that Dryden filled. Spence, incidentally, switched from drums to rhythm guitar. The line-up of Casady, Kaukonen, Kantner, Slick, Balin and Dryden was probably the most successful, producing five albums and exhibiting the willingness to experiment absent from the later dollar-conscious and (therefore) more simplistic days of the Starship. This is best demonstrated by the Kaukonen/Casady/Dryden star turn on *Spayre Change*, a nine minute jam from *After Bathing At Baxters* (1967) Dryden no less interesting on *Bless Its Pointed Head* (1969) where he deftly rescued the band from an 18 carat cock-up on *Fat Angel*. Ostensibly after a row with Balin, Spencer Dryden left the band in 1970, when everything seemed to be going wrong anyway, to join New Riders Of The Purple Sage. NRPS were originally a country rock spin-off band from the Grateful Dead with Jerry Garcia, Phil Lesh and Micky Hart included in the line-up, who would usually play support on Dead gigs. The Dead's Columbia recording contract meant the departure of Lesh and Hart, replaced by Dave Torbert and Spencer Dryden respectively, although Garcia hung on for a while until Buddy Cage came in when Garcia's commitments became too great.

NRPS has always been a rather lack-lustre outfit since their reasonable debut album, Dryden content to sit tight and play simple with seemingly no desire to return to a more challenging environment, apart from the Seastones one-off album (see below) when the Grateful Dead met Stockhausen.

On record

Spencer Dryden is on all Airplane albums up to and including *Volunteers* (1969), essential listening along with *Baxters* and *Pointed Head*. Interestingly, the one Dryden song on Volunteers is *A Song For All Seasons*, an out and out country tune. Dryden was also on Paul Kantner's *Sunfighter* album (1971) and an album of experimental electronic music similar in approach to *What's Become Of The Baby* from Dead's *Aoxomoxoa* album with Ned Lagin, Phil Lesh, Jerry Garcia, Grace Slick, Micky Hart, Dave Crosby and David Freiberg.

Of all the NRPS albums, probably only *NRPS* (1971) and *Powerglide* (1972) are worth bothering about, although Dryden features on all of them.

Aynsley Dunbar

The best drummer to come out of Liverpool, Aynsley Dunbar reluctantly came South in 1966 to add a new dimension of virtuosity to John Mayall's Bluesbreakers after Hughie Flint left. Overall, this line-up with Dunbar, Mayall, John McVie and Peter Green was probably the best, having no weak links. To use up some studio time, Dunbar recorded a drum single called *Rubber Duck*. His brief sojourn with the Jeff Beck Group in 1967, had an important stabilising effect on an otherwise volatile and, occasionally, shambolic outfit, but Dunbar quickly moved on to form his own band, the Aynsley Dunbar Retaliation with keyboardist Victor Brox,

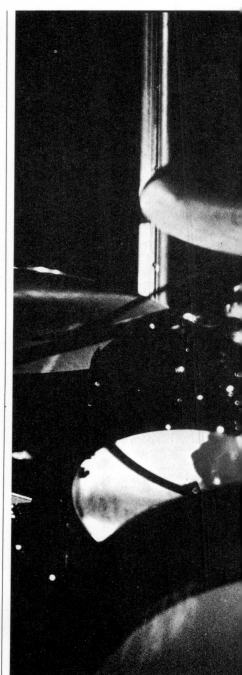

Alex Dmochowski (bass) and on guitar the ever sharp and tasteful John Morshead (who finished up in East Africa somewhere). Keyboardist Tommy Eyre was added later on.

Although firmly rooted in the British blues boom of the late Sixties, the Retaliation was more understated, muted, less raucous and less ponderous than some of its contemporaries. The jazz undercurrents were an important factor in this, coupled with the crucial fact that, unlike virtually every other out and out blues drummer,

Dunbar knew how to make blues swing and this gave a lighter feel to the whole sound, Brox's deep, raunchy vocals notwithstanding. When the band broke up, Dunbar tried an ambitious, but unsuccessful project called Blue Whale, with a brass section and under the pseudonym Junior Dunn, recorded an album with the British Sweet Pain including John O'Leary (ex-Savoy Brown harmonica player), Keith Tillman who had a spell with the Retaliation, John Mayall on bass and Dick Heckstall-Smith on sax.

However, feeling that the best opportunities lay in foreign climes, Dunbar moved to America to establish himself on the music scene there. It didn't take him very long – he was snapped up by Frank Zappa for the Mothers Of Invention, which signalled the beginning of an illustrious career as a band and session drummer in the States.

In 1973, guitar prodigy Neil Schon and keyboardist Gregg Rolie, who had made a big name for themselves with Santana, struck out on their own

Aynsley Dunbar

to form Journey. Their first drummer was Prairie Prince of the Tubes who played on a demo album that nobody heard, than left. Dunbar was recruited with Ross Valory on bass and for a short time, George Tickner on guitar. If this band had come together about three years earlier, they would have been a band of mega proportions – not through playing *schlock rock* but high calibre free form rock with long improvisitional passages.

The first album released in 1975 was a blockbuster, Dunbar's finest hour rumbling beneath Schon's blistering guitar work, lots of fine jazz cymbal patterns mixed in with tumbling bass drum signatures. A classic exercise in how to make rock music *move.* The following two albums were uniformly excellent but by now the writing was on the wall. They were heroes on the West Coast but hardly anyone else had heard of them. As the era of heavy pop dawned, vocalist Steve Perry was drafted in, new management plans were laid and, as the bank balances rose, the excitement and interest sank. By the time the T Shirts went platinum, the music was redundant. Dunbar tried to adapt; with the arrival of Perry and producer Roy Thomas Baker, for the *Infinity* album (1978), "I decided now it's time to start playing like Mick Fleetwood and that's what I did on this album. I tried to play as simply as possible". But it didn't work out and Dunbar left the band in 1979. However, for drummers in America anyway, the die was cast, simplicity was the order of the day, fill ins were for dentists and Dunbar, maintaining his astonishing record for landing on his feet, joined Jefferson Starship, but I won't hold that against him, even though he is my favourite drummer.

On record

Dunbar has contributed significantly to many fine albums, including: *Hard Road* (1967) John Mayall, *Aynsley Dunbar Retaliation* (1968), *Doctor Dunbar's Prescription* (1969), *To Mum From Aynsley And The Boys* (1969). (Interesting fact: The original line-up of the Retaliation was Dunbar, Peter Green, Jack Bruce and Rod Stewart – one track survives on an anthology of British Blues released in 1973), *Live At Fillmore East* (1971), *Just Another Band From L.A.* (1972), *The Grand Wazoo* (1972), *Waka Jawaka* (1972), *Chunga's Revenge* (1970), *Apostrophe* (1974) – all by Frank Zappa, *Pin-ups* David Bowie (1973), *Nine On A Ten Scale* Sammy Hagar (1976), *Berlin* Lou Reed (1973), *Slaughter On Tenth Avenue* Mick Ronson (1974), *Nils Lofgren* (1975), *Journey* (1975), *Look Into The Future* (1976), *Next* (1977) – all by Journey.

Sly Dunbar

Sly Dunbar and his inseparable cohort bassist Robbie Shakespeare, have emerged as the most important reggae musicians and producers

helping to break the music through to a wider rock audience and in the process becoming in-demand musicians for artists like Joe Cocker, Ian Drury and Joan Armatrading.

Dunbar is the latest and possibly greatest, in a line of distinguished reggae drummers such as Carlton Barratt, Michael Richard, Paul Douglas and Winston Grennan, laying down scintillatingly sparse rhythms with thick slabs of reverb and restrained use of syndrum, making its appearance in a song the more effective.

A session musician from way back, Sly Dunbar formed Work, Sound and Power with Robbie Shakespeare, which became Peter Tosh's backing band, and their own record label Taxi. Together, they have produced hits for Gregory Isaacs, Peter Tosh and Black Uhuru. The arrival of Sly and Robbie into the musical career of Grace Jones, resulted in her biggest selling albums to date, *Warm Leatherette* (1980) and *Night Clubbing* (1981). Now virtually synonymous with the word reggae, Sly Dunbar has been involved with just about every important artist on the scene, as the selected list indicates and is the most influential reggae drummer around, whose ideas are endlessly copied.

On record

Red (1981), *Tear It Up* (1982) by Black Uhuru, *Visions* Dennis Brown (1978), *Cumbalo* Culture (1979), *Rasta Communication* Keith Hudson (1978), *Planet Earth* (1978) & *Tell Me What's Wrong* (1980) by the Mighty Diamonds, *Long Life* Prince Far I (1978), *Equal Rights* (1979) & *Mystic Man* (1979) by Peter Tosh, also *Don't Look Back* by Peter Tosh and Mick Jagger.

Roger Earl

Roger Earl was with Savoy Brown during their most successful period at

the height of the British blues boom. From a musical standpoint (and through countless personnel changes), they shifted their style from a strict blues format to Chuck Berry-inspired blues boogie material. While they only packed clubs in Britain, they packed concert halls in America and it was there that Earl, guitarist Dave Peverett and bassist Tony Stevens quit the band to form Foghat. What Earl and Co. did was to cleverly build on the solid support that Savoy Brown had earned and develop the heavy chunky sounds of latter day Brown that were proving so popular. The net results were sell-out concerts, hit singles and gold albums; Willie Dixon's *I Just Want To Make Love To You* and *What A Shame* and the *Energized* (1974) and *Rock and Roll Outlaws* (1975) albums.

On record

Roger Earl can be heard on the following Savoy Brown albums: *Getting To The Point* (1968), *Blue Matter* (1968), containing the band's *pièce de résistance Train to Nowhere, A Step Further* (1969), *Raw Sienna* (1970) and *Looking In* (1970).

The last three albums can be regarded as transitional works linking Savoy Brown's blues antecedents and Foghat's more metallic boogey sound. Earl, a better rock than blues drummer, is on all Foghat albums from *Foghat* (1972) onwards and is heard to particularly good effect on *Rock and Roll Outlaws* (1975), *Energized* (1974), *Night Shift* (1977) and *Live* (1977), the meaty drum sound courtesy of Ludwig.

Bobby Elliott

Through the history of popular music over the last 20 years or so, bands operating in the mainstream pop scene have never been exactly noted for their individual virtuosity – least of all drummers, at best workmanlike, required only to keep time and lay down a steady beat. One of the few exceptions to the litany of uninspired pop drummers has been Bobby Elliott of the Hollies. Arguably the best musician in the band (and certainly the only one who ever won a Melody Maker poll – not just once but three years running), Elliott's unfussy but clean, precise drumming on tightly tuned percussion was inspirational to budding drummers of both the Sixties and the Seventies when, as some critics have claimed, the Hollies were producing even better material than before.

Elliott was not the Hollies original drummer – he swopped drum chairs with Don Rathbone, Elliott coming to the Hollies and Rathbone moving to Elliott's old job in Shane Fenton and the Fentones (aka Alvin Stardust). By that time, the Hollies second single a Coasters' number called *Searchin*, had reached a respectable twelfth spot in the UK charts. Then the hits started coming thick and fast and the band achieved international acclaim with such songs as *Look Through Any Window, On A Carousel, Bus Stop* and *Carrie Anne*, featuring some of Elliott's best work. He also made an unreleased drum record with Bob Henrit in the Sixties prior to Henrit's Argent days. The Hollies are still going strong – one of the most professional outfits in the business and Bobby Elliott remains what he has always been – a master craftsman.

On record

Hollies albums are legion but any greatest hits collection containing the tracks listed above is essential, e.g. *History of The Hollies* (1975).

Dennis Elliott

After kicking his way round the British second division rock scene for some years in relative obscurity, Dennis Elliott has now struck gold as Foreigner's man behind the traps.

In the Sixties he joined a soul-influenced band called Ferris Wheel with Linda Lewis and then changed tack by backing jazz-rock outfit If, who were constant visitors to America, which ironically probably prevented any UK breakthrough. There were sessions with Brett Marvin and Roy Young and a stint in the Hunter-Ronson band before he joined the instantly successful Foreigner.

On record

Can't Break The Habit (1967) & *Ferris Wheel* (1970) by Ferris Wheel, *If* (1970), *If 2/3/4* (1970-72) by If, *Ian Hunter* (1975) & *Overnight Angels* (1977) by Ian Hunter, *Foreigner* (1977), *Double Vision* (1978), *Head Games* (1979), *4* (1981) all by Foreigner.

Joe English

An American session drummer who joined Wings in 1975, (replacing Geoff Britton), staying with the band for nearly three years, which took in their staggering 13 month world tour, documented in the TV film *Wings*

Over The World. Jam Factory and Delaney and Bonnie had been part of English's dues playing period prior to joining Wings. Afterwards, it was back to the deep South and Chuck Leavall's band Sea Level. The former Allman's keyboardist was attempting what can best be described as blues/jazz fusion music which was only partially successful. English has since done some solo work.

On record

The Wings line-up that Joe English was part of, released *Venus And Mars* (1975), *Wings At The Speed Of Sound* (1976), *Wings Over America* (1977) and *London Town* (1978) and hit singles – *Silly Love Songs, Listen To What The Man Said, Let 'em In* and *Mull of Kintyre*.

While McCartney and his songs are obviously the keys to success in Wings (or failure as shown by *London Town*), and the focal points on any album, the strength of the overall musicianship should also be noted, particularly on *Venus And Mars* – solid material tightly supported at the back by some strong playing. English's Sea Level work comprises *On The Edge* (1978), *Long Walk On A Short Pier* (1979) and *Ballroom* (1980). He also appears on the Kingfish album *Trident* (1978) and released a solo album *Lights In The World* (1981).

Pete Erskine

Latest in a long line of exceptional percussionists for Weather Report, Erskine was a big band drummer with Stan Kenton and Maynard Ferguson and therefore a good choice for an ensemble structured on orchestral lines, able to 'swing' better than some of his predecessors. Erskine shows off all his chops on *Live In Japan* (1977 – particularly *Black Mark*) and *Night Passage* (1980) especially on the album's best track, *Fast City*. Also plays on Weather Report's *Mr. Gone* (1978) and their latest album, and features on side two of Joni Mitchell's *Mingus* (1979) in a more conventional jazz setting.

Victor Feldman

As a young drummer in the Fifties, Victor Feldman played on the British jazz scene in the company of luminaries like Ronnie Scott, Pete King and Benny Green. An aggressive musician in his playing style, he featured on an EP back in 1954 called *Seaman's Mission*, doing a drum battle with the legendary Phil Seamen. Feldman went on to find success as a vibes/percussionist in America and his large output includes: *Southbound* Hoyt Axton (1975), *Careless* Stephen Bishop (1976), *Reflections In Blue* Bobby Bland (1977), *Wild Child* Valerie Carter (1978), *Love Island* Deodato (1978), *Stampede* (1975) & *Living On The Fault Line* (1977) by the Doobie Brothers, *Rickie Lee Jones* (1979 – also plays vibes and drums), *L.A. Express* (1976) & *Shadow Play* (1976) by L.A. Express, *Righteous* Harvey Mandel (1969), *Groovin' You* Harvey Mason (1979), *Court And Spark* (1974), *Miles Of Aisles* (1974) & *Hissing Of Summer Lawns* (1975) all by Joni Mitchell, *Born Again* Randy Newman (1979), *Head Over Heels* Poco (1975), *Feel The Night* Lee Ritenour (1979), *Another Passage* Carly Simon (1976), *O My Love* Thijs Van Leer (1975), *Lumpy Gravy* Frank Zappa (1967).

Feldman has also worked with Phil Everly, the Four Tops, James Taylor, Allen Toussaint, Johnny Cash, B. B. King and played on every Steely Dan album, excluding *You Gotta Walk It* (1971).

Mick Fleetwood

One of rock's Nice Guys, a hard working, thoroughly professional drummer, who has come through many trials and tribulations to get where he is now, the major driving force both

on and off stage of the world's most successful rock band – Fleetwood Mac.

The original Fleetwood Mac line up of Fleetwood, Peter Green, Jeremy Spencer and Bob Brunning (i.e. no Mac!) came together in July 1967, but Mick Fleetwood's history goes back four years to the month before that date to July 1963 and a band called the Cheynes. According to those who saw them play, the Cheynes should have made it somewhere at the gritty end of the R&B market, alongside the Animals and the Yardbirds – but they didn't. And neither did the next three bands Mick Fleetwood was involved in; The Bo St. Runners, Peter B's Looners and Shotgun Express, the last one boasting Rod Stewart and Camel founding member, Peter Bardens (aka Peter B.) This brings us rapidly to Spring 1967 and Mick Fleetwood's four whole weeks with John Mayall's Bluesbreakers until he went the way of most Mayall sidemen.

Between 1967-1971 F. Mac lost Bob Brunning, Peter Green and Jeremy Spencer, gained John McVie and Christine Perfect and gained and lost Danny Kirwan, yet still managed to be Britain's best blues band. However, when the boom ended, Fleetwood Mac went into decline, the destabilising effect of further personnel changes making the situation worse. The nadir was reached in 1973-1974 when their manager sent a bogus Fleetwood Mac out on the road – the only people with smiles on their faces were the lawyers. After ten years in the business, Mick Fleetwood's career looked like a patient's chart after relapse – down-up-down. Had it all been worth it? And then came the biggest recovery in the history of rock – the arrival of the dynamic duo, Lindsey Buckingham and Stevie Nicks to help Fleetwood Mac produce exactly the music that America realised it wanted – wistful harmonies, soaring guitar licks and a down to earth rhythm – ideal for freeway driving.

Mick Fleetwood has no pretensions about his playing and probably smiled wryly when he and his long time colleague John McVie were heralded as the best rhythm section in rock by numerous critics, a standard accolade for fashionable musicians. In interviews he is proud of his innocence of technique – what he does, he does supremely well. What's

Previous page: Mick Fleetwood

more he can take great comfort from the fact that he's playing virtually the same as he was nearly twenty years ago, but getting paid substantially more for doing it.

On record

Rhiannon is still their best number and they are better on stage (where they can stretch out a bit) than on record – so what else could one recommend but *Rhiannon* on *Fleetwood Mac Live* (1981) – Mick Fleetwood's relentless beat on his Tama kit, taking the band to *Rhiannon*'s powerful climax.

D.J.Fontana

Elvis' first and best, if rather erratic and over ebullient drummer who joined Elvis when he first went on the road with Scotty Moore and Bill Black.

Fontana was also in on the first of Presley's RCA sessions on 10th January 1956, when *Heartbreak Hotel* was cut and he went on to contribute significantly to major hits like *All Shook Up, Don't Be Cruel, King Creole* and *Jailhouse Rock*, among others. Some critics, like Charlie Gillett, have claimed that Presley sold out his simple folk purity when he allowed RCA to put drums on his records, forcing him to inject false dramatics into the music in order to project over the increased volume. However, whether one accepts this or not, depends on whether you believe that Presley was at heart a "good ole boy" rather than a gut rocker. In any event, there were many reasons why Presley's career nose-dived artistically – drums were not one of them. Fontana's early savage rock style puts him up with the great rock drummers.

Steve Gadd

In some senses a redundant exercise

but nevertheless always stimulating for those interested in such matters, the question of who is the world's best drummer generally founders on the rocks of definition – best at what? Funk? Rock? Soul? Disco? Latin? Bebop? Jazz? Define your terms, man. Well, this question is much easier to answer nowadays since the emergence of a man who is not only the world's best drummer, but the world's best *DOZEN* drummers! Steve Gadd can do anything in any idiom from the most simple patterns to the most staggeringly complex and he can do them better than anyone else. Nobody even plays cowbell or hi-hat like this guy.

Born in 1945 in Rochester, New York, Gadd has been playing drums since he could walk – his drummer uncle gave him a pair of sticks when he was four. From seven, he had formal tuition from music professors of percussion, playing drum corps and orchestral music while at school. He also did a tap dance routine at a local club with his brother; tap dancing is actually recommended by Buddy Rich and Louis Bellson for developing bass drum pedal technique. He spent three years in the Army and then on to the Manhattan School of Music and the Eastman School of Music, before graduating with a degree in percussion.

Most of his early playing experience was on the jazz circuit often in the company of his school friends Chuck and Gap Mangione and also Chick Corea. Moving to New York in 1971, and determined not to sign to anyone, he made his way into the session scene to the point where he's on everybody's most wanted list; some artists wouldn't dream of recording an album without him. A man for all rhythms.

He is a quite remarkable drummer, able to do things other drummers cannot manage and playing with such power and conviction on every session, that the whole event takes on a new dimension; it is pushed to a higher level – he inspires artists both musically and emotionally. Top producer Phil Ramone says: "Steve Gadd is the best drummer in the world, the most musical. He is the most interested in your song and he hears it as a drummer. He's a songwriter's dream".

Apart from a packed diary of sessions, Steve Gadd has found time to record and tour with a session band called Stuff, sharing the drumming duties with Chris Parker and also featuring Cornell Dupree, Richard Tee, Gordon Edwards and Eric Gale.

Most of his studio work is done on a basic 4 drum custom built Yamaha kit using Steve Gadd black ebony drum sticks. Around London in the sixties, there used to be grafitti on the walls saying 'Clapton is God'. In New York nowadays, they write 'Steve Gadd for President'.

On record

This is difficult. It would probably be easier to list the people he hasn't played with, but a very select list looks like this: Stanley Clarke, Larry Coryell, Ron Carter, Chick Corea, Chuck Mangione, Bob James (first six albums), Deodato, Tom Scott, Art Farmer, the Brecker Brothers, Grover Washington Jnr., David Sanborn, George Benson, Earl Klugh, Lee Ritenour, Steve Kahn, Al Dimeola (all solo albums), Eric Gale, Larry Carlton, Hubert Laws, Al Jarreau, Van McCoy, Ben Sidran, Paul Simon, Phoebe Snow, Bonnie Raitt, Judy Collins, Steely Dan, Gladys Knight, Randy Crawford, Garland Jeffreys, Roberta Flack, Art Garfunkel, Rickie Lee Jones, Ringo Starr, Weather Report, Paul McCartney and Carly Simon (putting the venom into *You're So Vain*).

Of the dozens of albums he has played on, worthy of special mention are: *Tarantella (XIth Commandment Suite)* Chuck Mangione (1981), *Still Crazy After All These Years (50 Ways To Leave Your Lover)* Paul Simon (1975 – Gadd toured with Paul Simon and appears in the ONE TRICK PONY film), *Aja* (the title track, done in one take) Steely Dan (1977), *Leprechaun (Lenore)* Chick Corea (1976), *The Cat In The Hat (Seven Steps To Heaven)* Ben Sidran (1979 – a curse on the record company for not releasing this album in England), *Me Myself I* Charlie Mingus (1979 – of the drummers on this album, only Gadd keeps absolute time without so much as a flutter in the pulse), *The Captain's Journey* Lee Ritenour (1978 – just for the cowbell licks).

Bruce Gary

American session drummer who was only 16 when he was playing with blues guitarist Albert Collins. In 1970 he was a staff drummer with Capitol Records, copping licks from Louis Bellson who was doing big band sessions in the same building. He has worked with many leading artists, including Dr. John, Tim Rose and Jack Bruce, who he met at a Jim Keltner jam session. Subsequently he joined Bruce's regrettably short-lived band with Mick Taylor and Carla Bley in 1974 and its equally brief successor in 1975. Since then his gigs have included the revamped Love of 1978 and the Knack who recently broke up. Plays an unusual mix of Gretsch and Tama drums, Gretsch not particularly 'fashionable' among rock drummers.

On record

Bruce Gary's recorded work has included: *Puttin' On The Style* Lonnie Donegan (1977), *Slug Line* John Hiatt (1979), *You're The One* Rory Block (1978), *Thanks For The Music* The Giants (1976), *Hiding* Albert Lee (1979), *Get The Knack* (1979), *But The Little Girls Understand* (1980) both by The Knack.

Mike Giles

Mike Giles and brother Pete began an early association with guitarist Robert Fripp back in 1967 (Giles, Giles and Fripp) producing off-beat pop-oriented material on their one album and two singles which sold like bacon in Tel-Aviv. Pete became a solicitor's clerk, Greg Lake was prised away from a band called the Gods and together with Ian Macdonald, King Crimson was born. But Mike Giles' presence in the band was not as prolonged as avid Crimson fans would have wished. After the second album in 1970, he quit with Macdonald to do an American tour (which apparently put them both off touring for ever), plus an album and then went into session work. In this capacity he has played with everyone from Jack Jones to Roger Chapman, runs a Dorset studio called The Cottage and recently has reunited with Greg Lake for a new album.

But whatever he has done since, the Mike Giles legacy will be his extraordinary drumming on the first Crimson album *In The Court Of The Crimson King* (1969) – economic, inventive, lyrical and above all played with a sense of feeling possibly lacking in subsequent Crimson percussionists. It is a pity that a musician who made such an initial public impact should have disappeared from the public eye so rapidly, despite his many subsequent sessions (selected below). *21st Century Schizoid Man* featured in King Crimson's stage act after Giles left and in ELP's early live performances and no drummer ever did it better.

On record

Cheerful Insanity Giles, Giles and Fripp (1968), *In The Court Of The Crimson King* (1970) & *In The Wake Of Poseidon* (1970) by King Crimson, *McDonald & Giles* (1970 – excellent drumming on this album also Lee Jackson's post-Nice band, Jackson Heights), *5th Avenue Bus* (1972), *Ragamuffins Fool* (1973) & *Bump And Grind* (1973) all by Jackson Heights, *Silverbird* (1973), *Just A Boy* (1974) & *Another Year* (1975) all by Leo Sayer, *Confessions of Dr. Dream* Kevin Ayers (1974), *Butterfly Ball* Roger Glover (1974), *Graham Bonnett* (1977).

Jim Gordon

A very classy session drummer with a ton load of recordings under his belt – powerful yet tastefully restrained and controlled, master of the spare backdrop.

Output includes: *The Pretender* Jackson Browne (1976), *Out Of The Storm* Jack Bruce (1974), *Oh How We Danced* Jim Capaldi (1972), *Layla* Eric Clapton (1971), *Mad Dogs And Englishmen* Joe Cocker (1971), *Thanks I'll Eat It Here* Lowell George (1979), *Cry Tough* Nils Lofgren (1976), *Coming Out* Manhattan Transfer (1976), *No Secrets* Carly Simon (1972), *Pretzel Logic* Steely Dan (1974), *Cannons In The Rain* (1973), *Phoenix Concerts Live* (1974) & *In Concert* (1980) all by John Stewart.

Band stints for Gordon have included the Dillards, Derek and the Dominoes, the Souther Hillman Furay Band, Traffic and Joe Cocker, and other sessions have included Art Garfunkel, Neil Diamond, Alice Cooper, Freddie King, Elvin Bishop, George Harrison, John Lennon, John Sebastian, Frank Zappa, Gary Wright, Delaney and Bonnie and Dr. John.

Alan Gratzer

Founder member of REO Speedwagon back in 1968 which, with a dozen albums under its belt, has finally come into its own since the rise of 'Hard Pop' on the American music scene. By accident or design it's turned out to be the ideal compromise music – a rhythm section based in heavy rock with guitar solos to keep the headbangers happy *but* with pop-oriented melodies to satisfy the AOR market. The result – *You Can*

Tune A Piano But You Can't Tuna Fish (1978) with sales of over 2 million and *Hi-Infidelity* (1981) – No. 1 in the U.S. album charts for three months and sales for which there isn't a metal.

Gratzer is an unspectacular but competent, gutsy drummer whose kit by the modern standards of NASA – inspired hardware is positively miniscule – a wood shelled six piece Ludwig.

Ed Greene

Ed Greene is a top drawer L.A. session drummer with an enormous back catalogue of recording work to his name, the list below being very selective. Yet like many musicians in the session game, his name is hardly known outside the industry, not least because so much of his work goes uncredited on album sleeves, a practice which causes much bitterness among musicians who deserve to be treated better. Where would solo artists be without crack musicians behind them? Nowhere. Studio work can be a weird experience – for the Diana Ross session *Touch Me In The Morning*, Ed Greene never saw the star and on Donna Summer's *Last Dance*, he never even heard most of the music until it was on the radio.

Since working with Barry White, much of Greene's work has been with black recording artists, a testament to the esteem in which he is held, considering he isn't exactly a soul brother; Motown records have used him extensively. He is also working on a series of drum tutor records and plays a combination of Ludwig and Tama kits depending on the session.

On record

His California Album (1973), *Dreamer* (1974) & *Reflections In Blue* (1977) all by Bobby Bland, *Live And Learn* Elkie Brooks (1979), *The Contender* Jim Capaldi (1978), *The Cate Brothers* (1975), *Night Lights Harmony* The Four Tops (1974), *Sweet Vendetta* Adrian Gurvitz (1979), *Hall & Oates* (1975) & *Bigger Than Both Of Us* (1976) by Hall & Oates, *Pressure Drop* Robert Palmer (1975), *Having A Party* The Pointer Sisters (1978), *Love Breeze* Smokey Robinson (1978), *Touch Me In The Morning* Diana Ross (1973 – *for* the record and *on* the record, Ed Greene's name does not appear), *Aja* Steely Dan (1977), *Toussaint* Allen Toussaint (1971), *Rough* Tina Turner (1979).

John Guerin

Another West Coast heavyweight musician who has done sessions with the likes of George Shearing, Thelonius Monk, Elvis Presley, the Ventures, (including HAWAII 5-0 – remember that nifty drum intro?), Barbara Streisand, Hoyt Axton, the Byrds, Art Garfunkel, Seals and Croft, masses of TV work and the following selected recordings: *Be True To You* Eric Anderson (1975), *Diamonds And Rust* Joan Baez (1975), *Rich Man's Woman* Elkie Brooks (1975), *Dark Horse* George Harrison (1975), *Court And Spark* (1974), *Miles Of Aisles* (1974), *Hissing Of Summer Lawns* (1975), *Hejira* (1976), *Don Juan's Reckless Daughter* (1977) & *Mingus* (1979) all by Joni Mitchell. (John Guerin has been Joni Mitchell's most favoured drummer since her switch to more jazz-oriented material. The clarity of *Miles Of Aisles* is astonishing – every cymbal beat is crystal clear but all of Guerin's work with Joni Mitchell is recommended.) *L.A. Express* (1976) & *Shadowplay* (1976) by L.A. Express, *Gram Parsons* (1973), *King Kong* (1970) & *Canteloupe Island* (1976) by Jean Luc Ponty, *The Glow* Bonnie Raitt (1979), *Lumpy Gravy* (1967), *Chunga's Revenge* (1970), *Hot Rats* (1970 – particularly the title track) and *Apostrophe* (1974) all by Frank Zappa.

Plays Pearl drums.

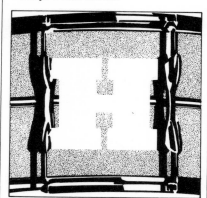

Micky Hart and Bill Kreutzmann

Where a band has two drummers on a regular basis who have the sort of empathy that Hart and Kreutzmann have, it is pointless to deal with them under separate headings. So as with

the Allmans, Doobies and Hawkwind entries in this book – the Grateful Dead duo will be discussed under one entry – this one.

In the early Sixties, Kreutzmann (aka Sommers), played with Robert 'Pigpen' McKernan in the Zodiacs. After Pigpen had teamed up with Jerry Garcia and persuaded him to change the band name from Mother McCree's Uptown Jug Champions to the Warlocks, Kreutzmann was recruited as drummer. The line-up stabilised at Garcia, Weir, Pigpen, Kreutzmann and Phil Lesh on bass, through the first two albums until Mickey Hart was brought in on percussion to Kreutzmann's initial chagrin, thinking Hart was after his job. In keeping with the group policy of individual member freedom, Kreutzmann has played with Keith and Donna Godchaux's jazz/R&B band.

Believe it or not, Mickey Hart learned most of his drumming chops from his *mother*, who at one time was a drum champion, as was his father. Hart came into the band in 1967 as a percussionist, gradually evolving into a second drummer on stage. Unfortunately, messy embezzlement allegations against the Dead's manager, also Hart's father, forced him out, but he rejoined later. He also opened his own studio, Rolling Thunder and plays in the Riga Rhythm Band. Kreutzmann and Hart complement each other superbly well, Kreutzmann the more rhythmic drummer, while Hart overlays the basic beats with textures of percussion. Both love to experiment in more free form playing around the central themes in any song. Most importantly, they are always aware of what the other is doing, sensitive to where the other wants to explore, where he wants to take the rhythms. The solos are musical conversations rather than battles.

Although both play drums (Sonor), Hart, as the percussionist, has a keen interest in all the drums of the world and has worked with ace Brazilian percussionist Airto, exchanging ideas and knowledge about South American and African percussion. Kreutzmann and Hart have constructed a huge rig called the Beast, from which are suspended steel drums, congas, marimbas, octobans and rototoms. Francis Ford Coppola was so taken with this astonishing edifice that he used it extensively for special effects work in APOCALYPSE NOW.

On record

The real worth of these two drummers to the Grateful Dead can only be appreciated live where the extended improvisational pieces allow for the generation of a whole range of percussive ideas to flow freely between each drummer. It was only on *Terrapin Station* (1977) that, using an outside producer, the drums were brought well up in the mix, not unlike the mix of Led Zeppelin albums. but probably their best attempt at demonstrating rhythm dynamics in the studio was on *Shakedown Street* (1978), produced by Lowell George.

Keef Hartley

Keef Hartley's career began in Liverpool in 1962 when he took over the vacancy in Rory Storm and the Hurricanes after a certain Richard Starkey went elsewhere. Two years later he came south to London to play in an R&B soul band led by Ron Wood's brother Art, which he ingeniously named the Artwoods with Jon Lord on keyboards. However, they never really took off (a name change to St. Valentine's Day Massacre sealed their fate) and when John Mayall asked Hartley to step in for Aynsley Dunbar, Hartley and the Artwoods parted company. The association didn't last long; the story goes that after a few months, Mayall suggested that Hartley should form his own band – but this was one of the leader's many ways of saying goodbye. The split was amusingly played out on record – the Mayall album *Bare Wires* (1968) had an instrumental track called *Hartley Quits* while on the first Keef Hartley album *Halfbreed* (1969), a telephone call from "John" is heard and plainly the news isn't good. The track was called *Sacked*. Adopting an American Indian persona in the mould of Mayall's own penchant for the prairie life, Keef Hartley formed what turned out to be a very fine jazz-blues outfit including Miller Anderson (guitar) the late Gary Thain (bass) and Mick Weaver (keyboards). When Hartley took a big band version on the road, the horn and woodwind section boasted some of Britain's finest – Henry Lowther, Harry Beckett, Lyn Dobson, Johnny Almond, Chris Mercer and Lyle Jenkins.

A lot of excellent music came from this band, Hartley leading from the front with tight, precise drumming and they were always popular on the club circuit, particularly The Marquee Club in London's West End. But there were internal dissentions exacerbated by taking a large group of musicians on the road and albums made after 1971 were largely done using session musicians. Between 1971 and the formation of Dog Soldier, a new band with old faces in 1974, Hartley had a brief reunion with John Mayall and spent the rest of the time with Michael Chapman in America. The return to Britain was not fruitful; Dog Soldier folded after one album and since then Hartley has done session work, opened a club in Kent and played the occasional gig.

Good music doesn't date and much of the Hartley product stands up to repeated listenings even more than ten years on.

On record

Diary of a Band Vol. I (1968) & *Diary of a Band Vol. II* (1968) by John Mayall, *Halfbreed* (1969), *Battle of NW6* (1970), *The Time Is Near* (1970), *Overdog* (1971), *Little Big Band* (1972), *Seventy Second Brave* (1973), *Lancashire Hustler* (1973) & *The Best of Keef Hartley* (1974) all by the Keef Hartley Band, *Dog Soldier* (1975). The first two albums are excellent, the rhythm and brass sections solidly meshed together overlain by Anderson's blues guitar. *The Best Of*, is a thoughtfully conceived resume of Keef Hartley's achievements), *Gallery* Artwoods (1964), *Millstone Grit* (1973), *Pleasures of the Street* (1975), *Savage Amusement* (1976) & *The Man Who Hated Mornings* (1978) all by Michael Chapman.

John Hartman

John Hartman, one of the founder members of the Doobie Brothers, originally came to California to try and reform Moby Grape with the West Coast's own Syd Barrett, Skip Spence. Instead, Spence introduced him to Tom Johnston and Dave Shogren and the three formed a hard rock band called Pud. Once the band had renamed themselves (Doobie being gnarled hippy slang for a cigarette containing certain substances) and signed themselves to Warner Brothers, they boosted their number to five, including a second percussionist Mike Hossack. This gave the band a two drummer line up technically similar to the Allmans, although "spiritually" they were closer to Moby Grape.

During 1973, Mike Hossack moved briefly to Bornaroo and played with Les Dudek, being replaced in the Doobies by Keith Knudsen, retaining the twin percussionists. The Hartman/Knudsen combination continued until recently when Hartman dropped out of the business altogether to become a vet and horse breeder. His place was taken by Charlie McCracken (see under Knudsen).

One is bound to say that having two drummers has done little for the band's sound on record, at any rate compared to the Allmans and the Grateful Dead – possibly because there are fewer possibilities for rhythmic experimentation. Therefore earlier Doobies albums were best, particularly *The Captain And Me* (1974) when the Doobies were a rock band rather than a pop band and still had the hard-driving sound epitomised by this album. John Hartman appears on all Doobies albums up to *Living On The Fault Line* (1977).

Roger Hawkins

Brilliant white R&B/soul drummer, who has been at the heart of the Muscle Shoals Rhythm Section working out of Muscle Shoals, Alabama for twenty years and now part owner of the MS Studio where he also produces. The original Fame studio was opened by Rick Hall in 1961 who proceeded to collect together the musicians he required to get the whole show on the road – Hawkins had previously seen service with the Delrays. When Hall signed Fame to an Atlantic distribution deal, legendary Atlantic producer Jerry Wexler came south, bringing his artists to record there – all time classics like *When A Man Loves A Woman* by Percy Sledge, *Mustang Sally* – Wilson Pickett and *Sweet Soul Music* – Arthur Conley. Other soul acts backed by Muscle Shoals included Solomon Burke, Aretha Franklin, Etta James, Don Covay and Bobby Womack and the rock list is as diverse as it is legendary. Hawkins played in an "unconfirmed" session with Presley in 1976 with other MS men, Cornell Dupree, Bill Payne and Lowell George, supposedly as the result of Colonel Tom Parker ringing Jerry Wexler to say "Mah boy wants to record with you!"

On record

The list of Hawkins credits with his Muscle Shoals compatriots would fill a book by themselves – they include: *Really* J. J. Cale (1972), *Boomers Story* Ry Cooder (1972), *Breakaway* Art

Garfunkel (1975), *Levon Helm* (1978), *Lovejoy* Albert King (1971), *Linda Ronstadt* (1972), *Boz Scaggs* (1969 – with the classic thirteen minute *Loan Me A Dime* during which Duane Allman throws in a breathtaking solo, while Hawkins engineers a 6/8 slow blues to a fast shuffle), *Night Moves* (1977), *Back in '72* (1972) & *Against The Wind* (1981) all by Bob Seger, *There Goes Rhymin' Simon* (1973), *Four* Billy Swan (1977), *Shoot Out At Fantasy Factory* Traffic (1973); also Millie Jackson, Laura Nyro, Cat Stevens, the Rolling Stones, Bob Dylan, Ronnie Hawkins, Jimmy Cliff, Lowell Fulson and Jim Capaldi.

Ritchie Hayward

Lynchpin of the characteristic New Orleans-inspired pulse generated by one of America's finest bands ever – Little Feat. Prior to joining the band, Hayward played in the Factory with Lowell George after the first drummer ran off to join the Moonies. The band, managed by Zappa overseer Herb Cohen, released one flop album before George split to do session work and the Factory continued as Fraternity of Man who left their mark as composers of *Don't Bogart That Joint* heard in the film EASY RIDER. Drumming wasn't Hayward's only job in the band. "I spent most of my time bailing them out of jail".

George had a short, stormy time with the Mothers of Invention after which he began to lay plans for Little Feat (the name is rumoured to have been a suggestion by Mothers' drummer Jimmy Carl Black in a reference to George's small shoe size).

From the band's formation in 1969 to the release of *Feat's Don't Fail Me Now,* (1974) they were virtually ignored by their recording company, Warner Brothers which, on more than one occasion, threatened the future of the band. During times of uncertainty, band members did session work; Hayward's gigs included John Cale's *Paris 1919* album (1973) and working for Ella Fitzgerald, Goldie Hawn and the Ike Turner band from which he was fired "I was too pale for them". He also had a bit part as Eddie Cochran's drummer in the film version of THE BUDDY HOLLY STORY.

Fortunately, with *Feats Don't Fail Me Now,* the band finally cracked it and they came to Britain in 1975 supporting the Doobie Brothers and

blew them out the window. From there they went from strength to strength musically but there was increasing dissention in the band, Lowell George was unhappy and in bad health. During the 1977-1979 period, Hayward, keyboardist Bill Payne and guitarist Paul Barrere were more and more influential while George was doing less and less but it is rubbish to talk of conspiracies against George as some have done since this death. Bill Payne quit in 1979 during the recording of *Down On the Farm* but left the door open for a reconciliation. Unfortunately it was not to be. At the time the break up was being announced, Lowell George collapsed and died while promoting his solo album *Thanks I'll Eat It Here.* The band was finished. Two weeks before George died, Ritchie Hayward broke a leg, Bill Payne commented 'it just seemed par for the course for the band".

But none of the trials and tribulations of this band should serve to detract from the fact that at their best there wasn't another band within striking distance, mainly because of the totality of their talent – they were superb in all departments. Beneath the immaculate vocals and slide playing of Lowell George and Bill Payne's swirling keyboards, there was an irresistible undulating sleazy funk rhythm courtesy of Hayward, percussionist Sam Clayton and bass player Kenny Gradney – a peerless interracial mix of New Orleans boogie and jazz, urban blues and white rock. Yes, the band had many internal problems but it is from such tensions that the most dynamic music comes; Little Feat's music was delicately balanced on a wire that threatened to snap – when it did, it was all over.

On record
It will come as no surprise if I say all Little Feat albums are recommended but if you are cast away alone on a desert island with the chance of taking one album to play on the system thoughtfully left by the last incumbent, then take *Waitin' For Columbus* (1978), a double live album that captures the lot. The rhythm section is amazing throughout but worth mentioning is Hayward's funky chops in a mini-solo during *Times Loves A Hero* and on *Feats Don't Fail Me Now.* If you win the pools, buy the half speed direct cut version which will put you in Row A of the front stalls. If two albums are allowed, take *Feats Don't*

Ritchie Hayward

Fail Me Now (1974) as well.

Ritchie Hayward has done a number of sessions with artists like Rick Nelson, Peter Frampton, Arlo Guthrie, Jackie Lomax, Carly Simon and Joan Armatrading plus; *Stephen Stills* (1970), *Ry Cooder* (1971), *Midnight Flight* Yvonne Elliman (1978), *Pressure Drop* (1975), *Some People Can Do What They Like* (1976) & *Double Trouble* (1978) all by Robert Palmer.

Heavy Metal

A genuine music subculture that refuses to go away. In spite of the almost universal slating that this music has come in for over the years, it's still with us and more bankable than ever – massive record sales, sell-out concerts and in Britain it's even got its own glossy magazine, KERRANG, boasting impressive circulation figures.

From a drumming point of view, (and from just about every other point of view), nothing has changed much since John Bonham, Cozy Powell and Ian Paice laid the ground rules back in the Sixties. In the current upswing of fortune, much of the drumming, particularly from the newer bands however, is predictable and over-flash, the idea seemingly that easy licks must be made to look difficult – and the best way to do that is to park yourself behind what Bill Bruford has dubbed 'a red sparkle child molester kit'. No HM drummer takes to the stage without a kit nearly big enough to shove the rest of the band into the front stalls – one drummer has appeared with 24 drums and 24 cymbals! Once set up and rolling, it's 'wallop everything in sight' which from a performance point of view is very important – not much to do with drumming, but everything to do with image. Now, the drummers listed below are all hard, powerful musicians who know their stuff, no slouches here. But 24 tom toms are not necessary to play heavy rock – the reason they are there, is because HM is rock on the grandest scale – fantasy, power, lights, smoke bombs, lasers, huge stacks and animated playing with much movement on stage. The drummer, however, is tied to one spot while he is playing, so the big kit is crucial to the projection of the *image* of the music as much as the music itself. By being big, flash and loud, the kit is more than just an instrument, it's a subcultural statement. More practi-

cally, for the less competent drummer it's a good insurance policy against making an idiot of yourself when rolling round the kit. Cobham's got a big kit, but he's just as devastating on a four piece.

And with the teenage market in mind – the drum companies love it; full page ads. along the lines of "Henry Headbanger of Lobotomy Express gets his kicks from the nuclear powered 50 drum Starflash Thunderbuck" – much better than the new wave/punk drummers who deliberately eschew all this, preferring the 20 year old Ajax with matching dustbin lids from Oxfam or the two by four drum machine that tucks in nicely next to sandwiches in the glove compartment. On the other hand, with equipment so horribly expensive, it's doubtful how effective drum endorsing or franchising is in boosting sales. (What the clever company does is to keep the same name on all kits through the range down to the cheapest so that the semi-pro can have the image of playing the same kit as his hero for considerably less money.)

The resurgence of HM revitalised old bands and threw up new ones reflected in the select listing below. Other drummers generally associated with HM have their own listing, like Neil Peart of Rush, either because they've got a bit more dues paying under their belt, or they are better, or both. One other distinction I would make, American HM drummers are better rockers than their British counterparts, too many of whom are just downright ponderous. It don't mean a thing if it ain't got swing – and that applies to Heavy Metal as much as anything else.

Ric Allen

Original member of the Sheffield-based band Def Leppard formed in 1978. *On Through The Night* (1980) was a good debut album, particularly *Rock Brigade*. Allen is one of the promising new breed of heavy rock drummers, following in the footsteps of the great as a Ludwig player. Unfortunately, the band as a whole, has suffered through insidious business manipulation which tended to take advantage of their immaturity, age-wise and business-wise. It is possible that the band will have to travel further down the rocky road before these young musicians individually or collectively can make their mark – they will then be older and hopefully, wiser.

Albert Bouchard

Known originally as Soft White Underbelly with Bouchard on drums, Blue Oyster Cult came together in 1970 under the guidance of rock critic Sandy Pearlman, who went on to become manager of Black Sabbath, among others. They developed a melodic/harmonic approach to heavy rock allowing for the display of more varied instrumental techniques, although there was no mistaking where this band were coming from on their archetypally named live album *On Your Feet Or On Your Knees* (1975). *Agents Of Fortune* (1976) and *Spectres* (1977) were two other excellent albums including their most noted track *The Reaper*. Always an interesting band, not content to settle firmly in one groove, they are unfortunately past their peak.

Clive Burr

Formerly with Samson, Burr coincidentally replaced Doug Samson in Iron Maiden. In their early days and through albums like *Iron Maiden* (1980) and *Killers* (1981), Burr had a tendency towards an "attack on sight" approach to drumming – hard and powerful but largely uncontrolled. There is much more evidence of control on their latest offering *Number Of The Beast* (1982) without any consequential loss of power.

Pete "Frank" Gill

The former Saxon drummer has had an unusual career for a musician most recently associated with HM, playing with the Stylistics and Jimmy James, as well as being one of the two drummers in the Gary Glitter Band. Using the hardware of the now defunct Italian drum company HiPercussion, Gill is heard to good effect on Saxon's *Strong Arm Of The Law* (1980). Gill has since switched to Pearl drums.

Nigel Glockler

Came in as Gill's replacement in Saxon having worked with Toyah Wilcox, Midge Ure, Bruce Woolley and Bernie Torme.

Joey Kramer

Aerosmith is virtually extinct but at one time it stood alongside Kiss as one of the main HM attractions in the States, without making much of an impact in the UK. Kramer did his best to try and pull together many of the patchy performances which per-

Joey Kramer

Alex Van Halen

Phil Taylor

vaded all their albums, keeping a tight rein on the rhythm lines. Therefore it is difficult to recommend any album, but *Greatest Hits* (1980) if you must.

Nico McBrain

McBrain was the driving force behind Pat Travers' dynamic opening salvoes in the HM field, *Pat Travers* (1976), *Makin' Magic* (1977) and *Puttin' It Straight* (1977). He was replaced by Tommy Aldridge and went on to take over from Jeannot Hanela in the French HM band Trust. McBrain has also done sessions with Stretch and Roger Chapman's Streetwalkers.

Andy Parker

Founder member of UFO back in 1970. Until the recent resurgence of HM in Britain, the band was virtually ignored here, garnering most of their acclaim abroad, notably in Germany and Japan. Parker is a fine drummer, fast, fluid and punchy, particularly on the excellent *Lights Out* (1977) with Michael Schenker.

Phil Rudd

The Sonor Drum Company manufacture really meaty, heavyweight hardware capable of withstanding heaps of punishment and probably few Sonor drummers put this to the test more than Phil Rudd, ever present member of AC/DC, one of the world's premier HM bands. They have taken America by storm and deservedly so, with piledriving albums like *Dirty Deeds Done Cheap* (1976), *Back In Black* (1980) and the very successful *For Those About To Rock* (1981). Guitarist Angus Young may be the

Levon Helm

centre of attention in AC/DC but the bedrock resides in the hands and feet of Phil Rudd.

Phil Taylor

Old Filthy himself – a Muppet Incarnate, an astonishingly tireless and totally manic drummer admirably suited to the mad dog mayhem of Motorhead which he drives from behind his Yamaha drums laid out claw-shaped around him. *No Sleep 'Til Hammersmith* (1981) is the one to endure. He doesn't play drums, he murders 'em.

Alex Van Halen

Drummer of Dutch descent with guess who (?) and a damn fine one at that within the confines of the HM genre – plays like he's got some spring in his limbs and not reinforced concrete. He sports the inevitable double bass drum set-up, but with a difference; each bass drum consists of two shells joined together by a concertina link, supported by steel rods. Unfortunately, it is impossible to determine the impact of this innovation on stage because of the incredible volume generated by the rest of the band. Excellent examples of Van Halen's drumming can be found on all their albums, but especially *Van Halen* (1978), their first album, where his approach is as confident and swaggering as his brother's guitar playing and David Lee Roth's vocals. Anxious to get in on the HM act, Van Halen has a penchant for kit leaping, in the style of Golden Earring's Cesar Zuiderwijk – perhaps it's something to do with windmills in the blood!

Levon Helm

The Band first came to the attention of the world during the Dylan tours of 1965-1966; they walked on to the stage as Dylan's backing band and left as stars. Levon Helm did not accompany them, staying in his Arkansas home until they got back – just one of the many mysteries surrounding rock's most private, most enigmatic, least interviewed group of musicians who gave notice of their intentions with the quiet arrogance of their name.

Helm started out in the Arkansas backwoods with a high school band, the Jungle Bush Beaters until a struggling rockabilly singer named Ronnie Hawkins took the teenager as part of his band up north to Canada where the competition was not so hot, leav-

ing Presley et al behind. Helm stayed as the rest of the band got homesick, to be replaced one by one with Canadians – Robbie Robertson, Rick Danko, Garth Hudson and Richard Manuel – and they played every flea hole in Canada as the Hawks, Levon and the Hawks, the Crackers and the Canadian Squires. Then Helm took Robertson back south to Arkansas and showed him the world that inspired Robertson's powerful sketches of American rural life. The rest followed, leaving Hawkins to ponder on the vagaries of life as Canada caught up with the rest of the North American music scene.

After the Dylan tours, Helm joined up with the others in a big pink house near Woodstock and began producing some astonishing music – songs that will endure, reflecting what they saw as the essence of America – complicated, dangerous and alive, wrenched from the guts and heart of one of rock's most expressive vocalists – Levon Helm. Even though many of Robertson's lyrics were obscure, the words sometimes difficult to catch, it was the *sound* that mattered, a creaky wind-swept world weary evocation of the American Dream. On songs like *The Weight* (written for Helm) and *The Night They Drove Old Dixie Down*, Helm was able to project searing emotion not only through his voice, but also through his drums; loose, fierce beats that were not just part of the technical rhythm of the song, but part of the imagery of the song itself – the drumbeats in "Dixie" *are* the drums of the Civil War they evoke. Few drummers have been able to integrate their drumming into the very soul of a song, born out of the strong empathy between band members and, more importantly, because Helm was singing the songs he was playing, allowing a physical as well as a spiritual interplay of voice and drums. In his great wisdom, critic Greil Marcus has said that Levon Helm is the only drummer who can make you cry – and I, for one, am not going to argue with that.

Since The Band officially broke up in 1976, Helm has been the only member to tour regularly, playing with the Cate Brothers. Danko and Helm have both done solo albums, Helm also signing himself to Muscle Shoals and starring in THE COALMINER'S DAUGHTER.

On record

It must be said that The Band put out some unsatisfactory albums by their own high standards – possibly too much was expected of them after their first two monumental albums, *Music From Big Pink* (1968) and *The Band* (1969), containing most of their best material. *Rock Of Ages* (1972) a live album and *Northern Lights, Southern Cross* (1975) are also excellent, as is one of their main albums with Dylan, *Before The Flood* (1974), another live album. *The Last Waltz* (1978), a triple live swansong with old friends was patchy; The Band were definitely the best on the night. Levon Helm's two solo albums were *Levon Helm And The RCO Allstars* (1977) and *Levon Helm* (1978).

Don Henley

If the voice of Levon Helm is the old steam locomotive chugging across prairie wastes, then Don Henley's of the Eagles is the smooth diesel, polished and tuned to perfection.

Texan born Henley came to California with his own band Shiloh in 1969 to cut a Kenny Rogers produced album in Los Angeles but lack of work forced the band to break up. During 1971, Henley and Glen Frey found themselves together in Linda Ronstadt's road band before teaming up with Randy Meisner (ex-Rick Nelson and Poco), Bernie Leadon (ex-Flying Burrito Brothers and Dillards) in the same year to form the Eagles, adding Don Felder a little later. The band was a success from the start, but dissatisfied with the move away from country to rock, Leadon left to be replaced by Joe Walsh and Meisner became a cattle rancher and occasional solo artist. Don Henley is quoted as saying that the theme of all Eagles' albums is "the quest". Well, whatever they were looking for (big houses in Hollywood?), they must have found because their music epitomises the Californian super-rich sound – sun-kissed *dreck*.

Henley has co-written much of the band's better material and is their best vocalist, particularly on their evocation of the rock band as outlaws *Desperado* (1973), an album that still had a satisfying roughness about it in places. In his day, Henley has brought some of Helm's power to the Eagles, enhanced by his songwriting capabilities. His vocals, rather than his drumming have been in demand and his sessions include Jackson Browne, Dan Fogelberg, Warron Zevon and Randy Newman.

Bob Henrit

Bob Henrit's career stretches back to the birth of British pop and rock with groups lost in the mists of time – Buster Meikle and the Daybreakers, Mike Berry and the Outlaws, Norman Eddy and the Imperials, Adam Faith and the Roulettes and Unit 4 + 2. Russ Ballard was in the latter three groups and it was ex-Zombie Rod Argent that kept them together, with his cousin Jim Rodford, in the band he formed in 1969 – Argent.

There were lots of good components in this band; Argent's keyboard playing, Ballard's song writing and Henrit's drumming which attracted the attention of many drummers. However, the whole was never as good as the individual parts and despite two hit singles *Hold Your Head Up* (1972) and *God Gave Rock And Roll To You* (1973), plus a brace of good albums, Argent could not haul themselves out of the second division. It was downhill after Ballard left in 1974 – the band stumbled on to 1976 when Rod Argent went solo and Verity, Henrit and Rodford formed Phoenix, cutting two albums with Argent and Ballard guesting on the second. Phoenix did a tour with Aerosmith memorable, apparently, for the fight which broke out between opposing band members and the subsequent refusal of either camp to speak to the other for the whole tour. Henrit also played in a band called Charlie which featured another drummer called Steve Gadd – but not *the* Steve Gadd. Once both Gadds were staying at the same hotel and reception went bananas transferring the wrong calls to the wrong room. Henrit has always been in great demand as a session drummer, his catalogue including Roger Daltrey, Colin Blunstone, Leo Sayer, Ian Matthews, Dave Davies and Don McLean during his recent British visit. A great enthusiast and very knowledgeable about drums, he has been involved in the music shop business and contributes to music magazines.

On record

Henrit was on all Argent albums, the best being *Argent* (1970) and *Ring Of Hands* (1971). *Daltrey* (1973) features Henrit and Ballard and was produced by their former boss Adam Faith. Phoenix albums; *Phoenix* (1976) and *In Full View* (1980). Charlie albums with Henrit – *Good Morning America* (1981) & *Here Comes Trouble* (1982).

Preston Heyman

Relatively new and impressive British drummer on the session scene. He has played in a varied cross-section of British bands since the mid-Seventies, including Carol Grimes, Brand X and Atomic Rooster and can be heard on: *Our Only Weapon Is Our Music* Gonzalez (1975), *In Your Mind* Bryan Ferry (1977), *TRB2* Tom Robinson Band (1979), *Never For Ever* Kate Bush (1980).

Jon Hiseman

Jon Hiseman is that rare combination of supremely accomplished musician and shrewd businessman whose bands have always attracted great in-

Jon Hiseman

terest among rock fans over the years, even though as a musician and bandleader, he has never quite attained the giddy heights his early career seemed to promise.

When Graham Bond noticed a young drummer rehearsing with the New Jazz Orchestra back in 1965, he made a mental note that if Ginger Baker ever left the Graham Bond Organisation, this guy was going to be his replacement.

In April 1966, that time arrived and Bond spent three weeks trying to persuade Hiseman to join him – Hiseman was then a semi-pro doing a day job as a trainee accountant with Unilever at £11 a week. The Bond promise of princely sums like £35 a week was the clincher. In any case, it was decision time for Hiseman – accountant or musician? He was working all day and playing all night in bands like the Wes Minster Five with Dave Greens-

lade on keyboards and Tony Reeves on bass, dance bands, jazz trios, the lot. He finally succumbed to Bond's persuasions and went on the road. Although the promised money never actually materialised, Hiseman built up a big reputation for himself playing with Graham Bond, well able to silence the sceptical Ginger Baker fans who came to watch this young drummer make a fool of himself behind a double bass drum kit. The Organisation line-up of this period – Bond, Hiseman, Dick Heckstall-Smith and a Nigerian horn player called Mike Falana, broke up in 1967 and Hiseman went briefly to the Georgie Fame band. One night he was invited to sit in for the second half of a Bond gig – in the audience was John Mayall. Shortly afterwards, Mayall sat in his car outside Hiseman's house for three hours waiting for the drummer to return, to ask him to join the Bluesbreak-

ers. This he did and was joined by Dick Heckstall-Smith and Tony Reeves with Mick Taylor on guitar. The new Mayall line-up which recorded *Bare Wires* (1968) was more of a jazz outfit than previous Mayall bands and this gave added impetus to an idea that Hiseman and Dick Heckstall-Smith had talked about during Organisation days – and that was to have a jazz-oriented rock band like the Organisation but without the lunacy and chaos.

The whole thing came together in 1968, when Dave Greenslade and guitarist Jim Roche joined Hiseman, Heckstall-Smith and Reeves in Colosseum. Roche was quickly replaced by James Litherland and other personnel changes during the band's three years history saw the arrival of guitarist Dave Clempson, bassist

Mark Clarke and Chris Farlowe.

At the time and in retrospect, the band was criticised for taking the ideas of the Organisation but leaving all the heart and passion behind, resulting in music that was too structured and complex and it must be said that the lack of musical "freedom" in the band was a major reason for its demise. But for the general record buying and concert going public, this band was a revelation. Nobody had ever seen anything like it before – powerful and dynamic ensemble jazz/rock which garnered them a considerable following in the UK. Every musician was a virtuoso on his instrument – the soaring runs of Dave Clempson, Dick Heckstall-Smith, the best blues saxophonist Britain has ever had and Hiseman's busy, rolling drums, precisely executed licks and fill-ins. The drum solo was the climax of the act, although this could be erratic – sometimes stunning, occasionally a nightmare, when Hiseman seemed to resent having to throw in the obvious crowd pleaser. But on their night (which was, often), they were a very exciting band to watch and when they broke up in 1970, Hiseman floundered for a while, unsure of what direction to take. He formed a more straight-ahead rock outfit called Tempest, using first Allan Holdsworth and then Ollie Halsall, both brilliant guitarists in different ways but neither happy in this environment. Lacking any real identity and purpose, they just blew long and loud, Hiseman did a solo and that was it.

Desultory and unsatisfying. Hiseman compromised his approach with his next venture, Colosseum II, still a rock band, but more inventive, more structured and not quite so totally dependent on Hiseman for its drive and inspiration. Hiseman brought together young, relatively unknown, but talented musicians like Gary Moore, (guitar), Don Airey (keyboards), Neil Murray (bass) and Mike Starrs (vocals) and together they made some tight interesting music. Hiseman was playing better than ever. But unfortunately, the late seventies was not the time to be playing this kind of music in the UK if you wanted to make any commercial headway and inevitably Colosseum II was unable to retain a stable line-up, losing Don Airey to Rainbow and Gary Moore to Thin Lizzy.

Hiseman must have come to the sad realisation that the rock business was just not interested in his style of music

anymore and that going through all the hassles of forming and trying to keep a band together just wasn't worth it. What he did was to move back into a jazzier environment with his wife, ace sax player Barbara Thompson, and her band Paraphernalia. In doing so, his drumming has become more controlled with the opportunity for more textural variations, percussive light and shade serving to heighten the drama of his playing. He still solos but it is now an integral part of the music, not the *de rigueur* climax of earlier days on which the success of the whole gig sometimes hinged. He did recently try to interest record companies in demo tapes he recorded with Jack Bruce and Allan Holdsworth. The reaction was predictable. "Nice music lads, but will it sell T-shirts?".

At the same time, Hiseman, always careful and intelligent in handling his business affairs, has developed his interests in other areas by becoming a promotional representative for Paiste cymbals. Often called upon for session work, he recorded Andrew Lloyd Webber's *Variations* (1977), now the theme for the South Bank Show and also the original soundtrack for the hit musical CATS (1981).

On record

The best of Jon Hiseman (and Colosseum as well) can be heard on: *Those Who Are About To Die* (1969), *Valentyne Suite* (1969), *Live* (1971) (The drum solo on *Daughter Of Time* (1970) is also excellent, particularly the bass drum work. Recorded live at the Albert Hall, it was part of the concert that Colosseum played as support to Steppenwolf after the Bath Festival and blew them off the stage), *Electric Savage* (1977), *Paraphernalia Live* (1980) – particularly the 5/4 solo on *Aliyah*.

Dave Holland

There once was a pop group called Pinkerton's Assorted Colours who had four singles released between 1965-1967. In a moment of daring and bravado, they dropped "Assorted" in an attempt to revive flagging fortunes – it didn't work.

Dave Holland re-emerged in Trapeze featuring Glenn Hughes later in the moribund Deep Purple of 1974. Trapeze was the only band signed to the Moody Blues Threshold label and their early John Lodge pro-

duced material betrayed this baleful influence. Things didn't improve when the band decided to become the new Iron Butterfly – it was just monotonous heavy rock. However, Holland's heavy metal destiny had been set – he played on Judas Priest's *British Steel* (1980) and has since replaced Les Binks in the band.

On record

Final Swing Trapeze (1974 – a collection of material from the first three albums).

Stix Hooper

In 1953, 15-year-old Nesbert 'Stix' Hooper put together a band called the Swingsters with his Houston schoolfriends Wilton Felder and Joe Sample – nearly thirty years on and thirty albums later, they are still together. They are the Crusaders – three gold albums as a band to their credit and, as the finest session musicians on the West Coast, contributors to over two hundred gold albums in the last ten years. The hard working, hard driving R&B-oriented Swingsters switched to being the Jazz Crusaders at the end of the fifties, playing free-form jazz, underpinned by Hooper's solid jazz rock rhythms. The move to playing funk was relatively painless; they tightened up, played more simple arrangements and dropped the prefix 'Jazz'. And it's been golden music ever since.

Hooper is wonderfully energetic but at the same time sparse player, always giving himself time to think about what he is doing, never afraid to slow down for fear of losing total control (one of the differences between a good drummer and a bad one). The Crusaders play like a well-greased machine but one that is engaging, soulful and beats with a human heart. Hooper plays a sprawling Pearl kit, his large 24inch bass drum punching through like a sledgehammer on record, with octoplus tunable drums, Pearl syncussion and a bristling array of cymbals. He released a solo album in 1979 called *World's Within* and at the same time, the Crusaders scored their major hit success with *Street Life*.

On record

Consistently excellent, Crusaders albums appear year after year, but to get a good overview of what a fine, exciting drummer Hooper is, one could do no better than the double *Best Of The Crusaders* (1976) in particular *Put It Where You Want It*,

Stomp And Back Dance and *Greasy Spoon.*

Mike Hugg

Manfred Mann started out as the Mann-Hugg Blues Brothers which despite the name was a jazz outfit formed around 1963. They followed the obvious trends in British music by becoming a five piece R&B band, the beginning of a run of 15 hit records in the next 5 years, including four Dylan songs, one of which *Mighty Quinn* gave them their third UK No. 1 in 1968. In the meantime, Hugg was flexing his not inconsiderable writing talents by composing the film score for UP THE JUNCTION.

Mann and Hugg split the band in 1969 to try something more ambitious – this was Chapter Three with a full horn section. They produced a creditable debut album, Hugg contributing an excellent version of The Yardbirds' *Shapes Of Things*, but the band didn't work out and folded in 1971.

Hugg went on to record some solo albums, passing up drums for

Dave Holland

keyboards and since then has concentrated on writing, particularly advertising jingles.

On record

The Manfred Mann catalogue is large; some twenty odd albums including compilations and Mike Hugg is on all of them. Also: *Up The Junction* (1968), *Chapter Three* (1969) & *Chapter Three Vol.2.* (1970) all by Chapter Three, *Somewhere* (1972) & *Stress & Strain* (1973) by Mike Hugg.

Ralph Humphrey

Tight, schooled drummer with excellent technique often used by Frank Zappa in the past as on *Hot Rats* (1970), *Overnight Sensation* (1973), *Apostrophe* (1974), and *Roxy And Elsewhere* (1974) which has some great licks from Humphrey and Chester Thompson. Tasty opening statement on *Sister Jo* from Gap Mangione's *Suite Lady* (1978).

Conrad Isidore

Experienced drummer whose work includes: *One* (1969), *Chapter 3 Vol.2* (1970), *Stephen Stills* (1970), *Stephen Stills Two* (1971 – the first Stills album was his best solo effort – Isidore played some spirited stuff on the album's best song *Old Times, Good Times*, contrasting with the sluggish Dallas Taylor on other tracks), *Vinegar Joe* (1970), *River* Terry Reid (1973), *Fathoms Deep* Linda Lewis (1973), *Back Street Crawler* Paul Kossoff (1973), *Hummingbird* (1975 – superb band formed by ex-Jeff Beck sidemen Bob Tench (vocals), Clive Chapman (bass) and Max Middleton (keyboards) with Isidore and guitarist Bernie Holland. After Isidore left, Bernard Purdie stepped in).

Reg Isidore

Brother of aforementioned Conrad, who played with Quiver before joining the original Robin Trower band playing on *Twice Removed From Yesterday* (1973) and *Bridge of Sighs* (1974). Since being replaced by Bill Lordan, Isidore's sessions have included Peter Green's comeback album *In The Skies* (1979), but he re-

appeared with Robin Trower on his latest album *Truce* (1982) with Jack Bruce.

Al Jackson

Probably one of the steadiest, most relentless time keepers since the first snare was cracked, Al Jackson was the granite, rock-steady base of the Mar-Keys and Booker T. and the MGs, the latter recording hit songs like *Green Onions, Red Beans And Rice* and *Chinese Checkers*. Members from both bands – bassist Donald Duck Dunn, guitarist Steve Cropper, Booker T. Jones himself and Al Jackson were also Stax session musicians during the sixties, contributing immeasurably to the hits that flowed from the Memphis studio, such as *Private Number, Walkin' The Dog, In The Midnight Hour, Dock Of The Bay, Knock On Wood, I Take What I Want, You Don't Know Like I Know* and many others. *In The Midnight Hour* is particularly interesting because at producer Jerry Wexler's suggestion, Al Jackson changed the habits of a lifetime and switched the drum accents from the weak 1 and 3 beats to the strong 2 and 4 beats, allowing Duck Dunn to play more melody lines. Because of the subliminally restrained and simple drumming on all these classic records, it is hard to realise just how Jackson made them sound so good. Maybe it was just his philosophy "it's the song that sells not anything else", that guided him as to what to do and when to do it.

When the MGs broke up, Jackson stayed in Memphis backing Al Green in particular, and also worked with Leon Russell, Rod Stewart and Eric Clapton. His long and illustrious career was tragically cut short in October 1975, when he was killed during a robbery at his home.

On record

Jackson's work with Booker T. and on the records mentioned above, represented the pinnacle of his career but he also contributed to Albert King's best albums, *Live Wire Blues Power* (1968), *Does The King Thing* (1968) and *Years Gone By* (1969). Also *Texas Cannonball* Freddie King (1972), *461 Ocean Boulevard* Eric Clapton (1974), *Night On The Town* Rod Stewart (1975).

Jaimo Johnson and Butch Trucks

The Y Teens, the Shufflers, the Escorts, the House Rockers, the Untils, the Five Minutes, the Hour Glass, the 31st Of February and the Allman Joys all have one thing in common – they were bands run by the Allman Brothers prior to the formation of the first Allman Brothers Band proper in 1969 with Butch Trucks and Jai Johnny Johanson (or Jaimo Johnson for short).

Butch Trucks had been in the 31st Of February and was a long standing friend of The Allmans from foot-slogging days around the clubs of Southern Florida, sometimes depping in other Allman bands in between gigs with his own outfit the Bitter End.

Duane Allman met Jaimo Johnson at Fame Studios, Muscle Shoals on the session for Wilson Pickett's *Hey Jude* (the singer refusing to say what he originally thought was 'Hey Jew'!). Johnson had also played with numerous other soul artists, including Percy Sledge and Otis Redding.

Between them, they had played just about every idiom in the book before coming together in the Allmans; jazz, R&B, soul, country and blues and the most effective two drum combo in rock brought all this wide-ranging experience to bear on one of the best Southern boogie bands ever. They provided a ferocious percussive thrust to the band, sometimes attacking directly into the melody, sometimes bubbling under, keeping everything on the boil and cooking, while Duane Allman and Dicky Betts took off on their extraordinary flights of guitar interplay. At other times, the whole rhythmic edifice of drums and congas would lay delicate and unobtrusive, gliding through the whole palette of rhythmic colours.

Trucks and Johnson rejoined the Allmans after periods in Trucks and Sea Level respectively, but Johnson left again in 1979.

On record

They played together for ten years and built up an awesome understanding in that time. Fortunately, they managed to capture much of their fine work on record, even the studio albums, unlike Mickey Hart and Bill Kreutzmann of the Grateful Dead. Having said that, the Allmans finest statement was the double *Live At Fillmore East* (1971) with the astonishing *Mountain Jam*, which reappears on *Eat A Peach* (1972), another double. The best studio albums were the first two *The Allman Brothers Band* (1969) and *Idlewild South* (1970) thoughtfully re-packaged as *Beginnings* (1973).

The Allman Brothers produced a unique brand of inspirational fusion music that is gone forever. Tracks like *Whipping Post* could be the jump-off point for jams that could go on for hours. But amazingly, the Allmans never meandered however long they played – the rhythm section saw to that – everything counted and nothing was spare. There were many comparisons to be made between the Allmans and the Dead and this was one of them, as an earful of the music demonstrates.

Kenney Jones

Kenney (or Kenny as he used to be known) Jones' career started out in Barry in South Wales with a group called the Outcasts with Ronnie Lane, going on to the Pioneers, again with Lane until the Small faces were formed in 1965.

A highly successful mod pop group (who unlike the Who, really *were* mods), only two out of fourteen singles failed to make the top forty. Their album *Ogden's Nut Gone Flake* (1968) was a psychedelic concept album, now regarded as a classic and spoken of in the same breath as *Sgt. Pepper*. However, their smooth magazine/recording image belied what a bunch of hard rockers they really were and the break up of the group in 1969 was followed by the formation of two bands very much in this mould, Humble Pie (Steve Marriott) and The Faces (Lane, Jones and Ian McLagan). Together with Rod Stewart and Ron Wood, the Faces were a premier 'good-time' live band, whose knockabout approach did not carry over to the studio and on record, Rod Stewart as a solo artist fared much better. But on stage, there probably wasn't a band to touch them.

The Small Faces reunion which followed the break-up of The Faces in 1975 after a good six year run, was a travesty – things were looking none too good for Kenney Jones and he almost gave up playing completely when the call came to fill the vast abyss in the Who, resulting from the death of Keith Moon.

The fates of Moon and Jones had been quite closely linked over the years. When the Small Faces and the Who were the main mod bands on the London scene, the two drummers had loomed about a lot together – they remained good friends and Jones played on the soundtrack of the film TOMMY. One of the first things Kenney Jones did when he joined the Who, was to order a large Premier kit decorated with hunting scenes, reminiscent of Keith Moon's famous *Pictures Of Lily* kit, made for him by Premier in the late sixties.

The drumming styles of Moon and Jones could not be more contrasting, one a cyclonic drummer who created whirlwinds of sound, the other rock-steady and comparatively unspectacular, a good loud rocking drummer, as shown on *You Better You Bet* from *Face Dances* (1981), Jones' first Who album. Although not a totally satisfactory album, it does have a more controlled, less manic feel about it, due no doubt, to Jones' calming rhythmic influence.

On record

Kenney Jones session gigs have included: *Joan Armatrading* (1976) & *Show Some Emotion* (1977) by Joan Armatrading, *La Booga Rooga* Andy Fairweather Low (1975), *It's Only Rock'n'Roll* Rolling Stones (1974), *Gasoline Alley* (1970) & *Never A Dull Moment* (1972) by Rod Stewart.

The most satisfactory Faces' albums were: *Long Player* (1971) and *Nod's As Good As A Wink* (1972).

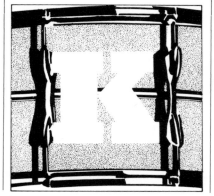

Jim Keltner

One of the world's top rock session drummers, part of the Jim Gordon/Jeff Porcaro/Rick Marotta/Russ Kunkel 'Mafia', who seem to have the rock scene sown up, allowing for the fact that Steve Gadd has every scene sown up.

After a long spell in jazz, Keltner kicked off his rock career with Delaney Bramlett in 1969 and the Joe Cocker 'Mad Dogs' tour of 1970. Since then, he has played with John Lennon and Ringo Star (including the Bangla Desh gig with both Keltner and Starr on stage). For the last two years he has been Bob Dylan's tour drummer and was in the Ry Cooder band for the May-June 1982 visit to the UK. During 1975-1977 he had his own band Attitudes with Danny Kortchmar, which is now defunct due to the recording commitments of individual band members. Plays a black Steve Gadd style Yamaha kit, but has recently been bowled over by the new Simmons SDS V electronic kit.

On record

The Keltner catalogue includes: *Out Of The Storm* Jack Bruce (1974), *Mad Dogs And Englishmen* Joe Cocker (1971), *Into The Purple Valley* (1972), *Boomers Story* (1972), *Paradise and Lunch* (1974 – Keltner at his stunning best), *Chicken Skin Music* (1976), *Bop 'Til You Drop* (1979), *Borderline* (1980) & *The Long Riders* (1980) all by Ry Cooder, *Shades* J. J. Cale (1981), *Lady's Not For Sale* (1972) & *Satisfied* (1979) by Rita Coolidge, *Ghost Town Parade* Les Dudek (1978), *Pat Garratt & Billy The Kid* Bob Dylan (1973), *Bangla Desh Concert* George Harrison (1972), *Attitudes* (1975) & *Good News* (1977) by Attitudes, *Ringo* (1973) & *Rotogravure* (1976) by Ringo Starr.

Other sessions: James Taylor, B. B. King, Gary Wright, Carly Simon, Yoko Ono, Randy Newman, Leon Russell, Dan Fogelberg, Lowell George, Jackson Browne, Booker T. and Alice Cooper.

Lee Kerslake

Uriah Heep drummer with an interesting history going back to a band called The Gods in the summer of '67 with Ken Hensley and Greg Lake and also at various times Mick Taylor and

Overleaf: Lee Kerslake

the late ex-Tull bassist John Glascock who died tragically in 1979. Both Kerslake and Hensley reappeared in Cliff Bennett's band Toefat, until Kerslake got himself fired. Formed initially in 1969, Heep went through three drummers including Nigel Olsson on loan from Elton John before Kerslake finally joined in 1971. During that year, his own National Head Band had folded. Kerslake survived umpteen personnel changes in Heep until 1981 when he joined crooning balladeer Ozzy Osbourne in Blizzard of Ozz; Tommy Aldridge has since taken over and Kerslake has returned to Heep.

Even for a heavy rock band, seldom has such universal scorn and yak droppings been dumped on the heads of a set of musicians – one critic commented "if this group makes it, I'll have to commit suicide". With sell-out concerts and two gold albums here and in America, Heep had more than enough money to send a bunch of daffs to the funeral. It is a commonplace to record Heep as one of the worst bands ever to have succeeded – American critics being particularly vitriolic.

On record

Genesis (1968) & *To Samuel A Son* (1970) by The Gods, *Toefat* (1970), *Albert One* National Head Band (1971), *Proud Words On A Dusty Shelf* Ken Hensley (1973), *Take No Prisoners* David Byron (1975), *Uriah Heep* (all Heep albums from *Demons & Wizards* (1972) to *Fallen Angel* (1978)), *Blizzard Of Ozz* (1980) & *Diary Of A Madman* Ozzy Osbourne (1981).

I make no comment about Heep – you either love 'em or hate 'em.

Simon King and Alan Powell

Between 1974-1977, King and Powell were the twin-drum powerhouse of Hawkwind.

Simon King came into the band replacing Terry Ollis early in 1972; the band had a lot of respect for Ollis who had taken lessons from Phil Seaman but couldn't really keep up with the heavy touring schedule. King had already been in a short-lived enterprise with Lemmy called Opal Butterfly. Powell came in as a deputy for King when he was injured playing football but stayed to become the band's second drummer. Powell had previously seen service with Chicken

Shack, Vinegar Joe and Stackridge.

During the King/Powell period, Hawkwind released *Warrior On The Edge Of Time* (1975) and *Astounding Sounds And Amazing Music* (1976) and both drummers appeared on *New Worlds Fair* (1975) by Michael Moorcock and Deep Fix.

Alan Powell and bassist Paul Rudolph got their marching orders for apparently trying to make Hawkwind FUNKY (gasp!) and went off to form Kicks. Since then Powell has appeared on: *Vampires Stole My Lunch* Mick Farren (1978), *The Korgis* (1979), and played with Tanz Der Youth.

Simon King left the band in 1981 and Ginger Baker plays on *Sonic Attack* (1981).

Simon Kirke

A very influential drummer in many respects, particularly for his economic, stripped down rock rhythms with Free, where he allowed Andy Fraser to weave his intricate bass lines around Paul Kossoff's masterful nerve-tingling guitar – on the night they were something a bit special, a cut above yer average British rockers.

Kossoff and Kirke had been together in a band called Black Cat Bones; Paul Rodgers with the Roadrunners (including Mick Moody ex-Whitesnake) and Brown Sugar while Andy Fraser had arrived from John Mayall's Bluesbreakers. Alexis Korner gave them early encouragement and their name.

The band split up in May 1971 and reformed again in January 1972, finally calling it a day in July 1973 by which time Andy Fraser had already gone to Sharks. Rodgers and Kirke found instant megastardom with Bad Company, Kirke carrying on in the same effective vein but despite financial success they were never as good as Free. Peter Grant used to let Bad Company out now and again but they've been underground for ages, although Kirke guests on Jim Capaldi's *Let The Thunder Cry* (1981).

On record

Barbed Wire Sandwich Black Cat Bones (1970), *Tons Of Sobs* (1969), *Free* (1969), *Fire & Water* (1970), *Highway* (1970), *Live* (1971) & *The Free Story* (1973) all by Free. (Free produced some great material *Mr. Big, The Hunter, Fire And Water, The Stealer, Ridin' On A Pony, Be My Friend* and the classic *All Right Now,*

without which no party is complete. Listening to some of Whitesnake's songs, the similarities are remarkable, particularly on slower numbers like *Carry Your Load* on *Ready And Willing* (1980) and *Blindman* from the same album – there is even a line that goes "be my friend/be my brother"!), *Kossoff, Kirke, Tetsu and Rabbit* (1971 – a studio album made during Free's interregnum and undistinguished apart from one ace track called *I'm On The Run*. Worth digging out of the 50p. remainder racks just for this song), *Bad Company* (1974), *Straight Shooter* (1975), *Run With The Pack* (1976). (Good stuff but much the same as before, except more lucrative).

Keith Knudsen and Chet McCracken

Keith Knudsen came into The Doobies as replacement for Mike Hossack having previously played in the Lee Michaels Band. Master of the overdub, Michaels was also noted for his duet tours featuring himself on organ and vocals and a huge drummer called Frosty (Bartholomew Smith-Frost); Knudsen metaphorically filled Frosty's shoes on *Space* and *First Takes* (1972) and *Nice Day For Something* (1973). McCracken had previously been with a hard rock outfit called Rare Earth.

He used to play a set of revolutionary North drums with the horn shaped shells that projected sound outwards instead of downwards. Unfortunately, they were unusable for stage work with The Doobies due to the miking arrangements for the band, so he switched to Ludwig. Knudsen plays Pearl, neither drummer uses a large kit – McCracken's is just a four-piece. This has its advantages in that it helps to ensure a fairly seamless rhythm sound with few temptations for over-complicated fill-ins, a temptation which Knudsen admits to.

Is it worth the Doobies having two drummers? Listen to *One Step Closer* (1980) and judge for yourself.

Knudsen is also moving into production while McCracken has plans for solo work. The future of the Doobies at the time of writing looks uncertain.

Russ Kunkel

If somebody could actually work out with total accuracy which rock drummer has done the most sessions, then this quintessential L.A. drummer would not be far short of No.1, if not THE No.1.

As a band/touring drummer, he was in the Steve Stills Band in 1974 and CSN&Y Mark 3 in 1974-75, as well as James Taylor's backing band with Carole King, Danny Kortchmar and Lee Sklar, which became The Section. Since 1972 they have recorded three albums of little merit.

Some of Kunkel's best chops can be heard on: *The Pretender* (1976) & *Running On Empty* (1978) by Jackson Browne, *Heartbreak Radio* Rita Coolidge (1981), *Souvenirs* Dan Fogelberg (1975), *Tapestry* Carole King (1972 – especially *Where You Lead*), *For The Roses* Joni Mitchell (1972), *Heart Like A Wheel* (1974) & *Prisoner In Disguise* (1975) by Linda Ronstadt, *Pat Garratt & Billy The Kid* Bob Dylan (1973), *Bombs Away Dream Babies* John Stewart (1979), *Excitable Boy* Warren Zevon (1978).

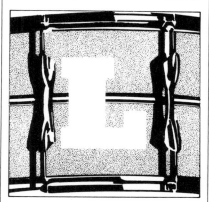

Corky Laing

A Canadian drummer who featured in two doomed attempts to recreate Cream.

The first was Mountain with Cream producer Felix Pappalardi (bass), Leslie West (guitar) and Steve Knight (keyboards). Laing replaced original drummer Norman D. Smart II, (who went on to do sessions with Gram Parsons and Todd Rungren), shortly after the band played Woodstock in August 1969.

Their albums sold well in America but not in Britain. Live they were horrendously loud but on record they were controlled, producing some

good music particularly *Flowers Of Evil* (1971) and *Mountain Live* (1972), with a long version of *Nantucket Sleighride*, actually more diverse and interesting than the comparable Cream extended jam on *Spoonful*. The studio version was on the album of the same name released in 1971. A later live double album *Twin Peaks* (1977) had a creditable version of the Pete Brown/Jack Bruce classic *Theme For An Imaginary Western*, one of the finest songs about rock music ever written (and one of the finest rock songs ever written, if it comes to that). The album's low point, however, was an interminable version of *Nantucket Sleighride* taking up a side and half. Ugh!

Once Pappalardi returned to studio work West, Bruce and Laing emerged – an abomination from first to last, Pete Frame changed the group name to Why Bother Lads and that just about sums it up. Corky Laing recorded a solo album *Makin' It On The Street* (1977) – I assume he means the album because that's what it sounds like.

Two awards to be made: 1) West, Bruce and Laing albums – for the most times spotted in remainder racks. For the masochistic among us; *Why Dontcha* (1972), *What Ever Turns You On* (1973), *Live and Kickin'* (1974). 2) Corky Laing – for most sticks dropped during a concert – Rainbow Theatre, London 1973. Then again he could afford to – 'Corky Laing' sticks were a very successful product in their day and Laing used to buy 250 pairs at one go.

Martin Lamble

Original drummer with Fairport Convention on their first three albums, *Fairport Convention* (1968), *What We Did On Our Holidays* (1969) and *Unhalfbricking* (1969). A genial guy, given to wearing an alarm clock round his neck, he was tragically killed in a road accident in June 1969 when the group's van crashed on the motorway. Also killed in the crash was an American clothes designer, Jeanie 'The Tailor', to whom Jack Bruce dedicated his debut solo album *Songs For A Tailor* (1969). Lamble's death put the group's future in doubt for quite some time.

Gilson Lavis

A good example of a musician who has been around a fair time before becoming an "overnight success" – the band in this case being Squeeze. An excellent drummer who plays with a lot of fire and confidence, he started out in a Sixties band called Headline News, one of the many troops of aspiring lads who found out the hard way what gigging round Europe was all about. He toured with some big name artists like Chuck Berry, Jerry Lee Lewis and George Hamilton, turning up one year at the Wembley Country Music Festival. He tried his hand at running a music shop in Southend, formed a country band called Beaver, worked in a brickyard and then joined Squeeze, playing on all their albums to date since the first one in 1978.

Lavis is dynamic and powerful both on stage and on record; tracks like *Tempted* and *Yap Yap Yap* on *East Side Story* (1981), (also the tracks on a single) the first with a Phil Colling/Jerry Marotta feel from the Peter Gabriel album and the second, a straight rock and roll song both displaying fashionably sparse use of cymbals other than hi-hat. The latest Squeeze album *Sweets From A Stranger* (1982) is their most powerful offering yet, precisely because Lavis is more to the fore than on previous recordings.

Gaspar Lawal

Nigerian percussionist based in Britain, with vast experience from Vinegar Joe and Ginger Baker's Airforce to Barbra Streisand. He also released an album of solo material recently to widespread critical acclaim.

Sessions include: *Back To The Night* Joan Armatrading (1975), *It's Getting Better* Atlantis (1974), *First Base* (1972) & *Amar Cabellero* (1973) by Babe Ruth, *We Put Our Magick On You* Graham Bond (1971), *Nude Camel* (1981), *Seriously Speaking* (1975) & *Everyday* (1975) by Clancy, *Sonja Kristina* (1980), *Men Opening Umbrellas Ahead* Viv Stanshall (1974), *Stephen Stills Two* (1972).

Graham Lear

Drummers in America have been very impressed with this young Canadian drummer who replaced Mike

Shrieve in Santana. He is very much a Shrieve clone, making him an exceptionally talented musician; listening to *Moonflower* (1977), a live double album and the excellent *Zebop* (1981), it is hard to believe that Shrieve is not playing. Plucked from nowhere by Carlos Santana, Graham Lear deserves wider recognition.

Ric Lee

Ric Lee teamed up with Alvin Lee (no relation) and Leo Lyons to form the Jaybirds, adding Chick Churchill on keyboards and changing the name to Ten Years After in 1967.

Although part of the British blues boom, TYA were more rock and even jazz influenced with Woody Herman's *Woodchopper's Ball* featuring in their early stage act. They were a very big club draw in England, with a residency at The Marquee where they started out, but didn't really hit the big time until the Woodstock Festival of 1969 and the eleven minute version of Alvin Lee's masterpiece *Going Home*. This ensured the band's superstar status and they went on to do more tours of America than any other British group. Not surprisingly however, after years of constant touring, the whole enterprise started going very stale indeed and between 1973-1975 TYA's desultory appearances signalled the end, despite rumours and counter-rumours about the group's future. In retrospect, their Woodstock success stereotyped the band fatally at the same time as they were trying, albeit unsuccessfully, to change the format on record with electronic experimentation.

When the band came to its messy conclusion in 1973, almost 'ten years after' they had come together, Ric Lee and Leo Lyons went into production. However, Lee carried on playing, this time with the evergreen Stan Webb, helping to perpetuate THE MOUSETRAP of rock music – Chicken Shack, which despite never coming within light years of the success of other stayers like the Who, the Kinks and Floyd, only packed up early in 1982. Can this really be the end? We will have to wait and see.

Ric Lee always tended to be overshadowed in TYA, not only by Alvin Lee, but by Leo Lyons on bass, a positively demonic performer on stage, not to be underrated as a contributor

Corky Laing

to TYA's excellent visual styel. Nevertheless, Lee was an accomplished drummer with all the necessary chops, given his spotlight on such tracks as *Shantung Cabbage* from *Undead* (1968) and *The Hobbit* from *Recorded Live* (1973).

On record
Definitive TYA are to be found on their first three albums *Ten Years After* (1967), *Undead* (1968) and *Stonedhenge* (1969). *Undead* was a live album recorded at Klooks Kleek in North West London, now the Moonlight Club at The Railway Tavern.

Jaki Liebezeit

Drummer/percussionist with the German *avant-garde* rock band Can, since its formation in 1968. A very important Continental group, who have specialised in a sparse, hypnotic style of fractured rhythms and harmonies. Jaki Liebezeit's approach to simple pulse drumming has been endlessly copied by many of the new wave drummers, particularly in those bands with a leaning towards angular "teutonic" sounds.

On record
Tago Mago (1971), *Ege Bamyasi* (1972) and *Future Days* (1973) represent their best work. *Cannibalisms* (1978) is a "best of" collection.

Bill Lordan

A drummer with a wealth of top class experience, including Ray Charles, Ike and Tina Turner, Bobby Womack and Sly Stone. He replaced Reg Isidore in Robin Trower's band in 1975, bringing extra bite to the rhythm section, particularly on *For Earth Below* (1975) and *Long Misty Days* (1976). He stayed with Trower up to the first album with Jack Bruce, *BLT* (1981), but on *Truce* (1982), Isidore is back on drums.

Stan Lynch

After tough legal hassles with MCA, Tom Petty and the Heartbreakers broke through with *Damn The Torpedoes* (1979) racking up sales of over 2½ million, one of the outstanding features of the album being the drumming of Stan Lynch. Although he is basically a rock'n'roll drummer, his work contains elements of the old Motown sounds of Benny Benjamin and Euriel Jones. Using a Tama kit,

Lynch has a big, clean open sound which I suspect is mercifully free of gaffer tape and which is retained on *Hard Promises* (1981) despite Petty's move away from Springsteen influences to a softer, more introspective country/pop feel, reminiscent of the Byrds. Lynch is admirably adaptable, sensitive of Petty's mood changes between songs.

Jerry Marotta

Playing with Hall and Oates has helped this young drummer make his mark on the session scene, further enhanced by his work on Peter Gabriel's last album which also featured Phil Collins, although Marotta did most of the session. Drummers would have noticed the absence of cymbals on this album; an idea of Gabriel's, it took Marotta and Collins some getting used to, but the effect was to bring an eerie starkness to the album that played no small part in the tremendous impact this record made when it was released in 1980.

Rick Marotta

Jerry's older brother, self-taught Rick Marotta is a very much in demand session drummer with a natural feel for drumming which has compensated hugely for his lack of formal training. In 1970 he was with the Riverboat Soul Band which had an album on Mercury, followed in 1971 by the Brethren, a hot R&B soul band who often backed Island artists on tour in the States, like Joe Cocker and Traffic. Widely tipped for stardom, Brethren didn't make it and Marotta vowed never to work for anyone again, retreating into the studio and the inner tribe of session musicians. From then on, he built up a solid reputation in the business, used by Paul

Simon and John Lennon among others, until in 1977 he went on tour with Linda Ronstadt and played her *Simple Dreams* album of 1977. This propelled him even further into the limelight and he has been going from strength to strength. He also has his own rock 'n' roll outfit called Ronin, managed and produced by Peter Asher. Introduced to Yamaha drums by Steve Gadd, Rick Marotta can be heard on: *Come As You Are* Ashford and Simpson (1976), *Bride Stripped Bare* Bryan Ferry (1978), *Whirlwind* Andrew Gold (1980), *Abandoned Luncheonette* Hall and Oates (1973), *Mind Games* John Lennon (1973), *Sound Of A Drum* (1976) & *The Path* (1978) by Ralph McDonald, *Little Criminals* Randy Newman (1977), *The Glow* Ronnie Raitt (1979), *There Goes Rhymin' Simon* Paul Simon (1973), *Spy* (1979) & *Come Upstairs* (1980) by Carly Simon, *The Royal Scam* (1976) & *Aja* (1977) by Steely Dan, *Jasmine Nightdreams* Edgar Winter (1975), *Excitable Boy* Warren Zevon (1978).

John Marshall

A superb jazz/rock technician, John Marshall has been Soft Machine's drummer since Robert Wyatt left in 1972. However, while the band more than compensated for Wyatt's loss in technical and musical excellence, they could not really hope to replace his inspiration and their material declined in its imaginative quality after his departure. Prior to his Soft Machine commitments, Marshall had worked with many musicians in both the jazz and rock fields including Alexis Korner, Larry Coryell and Jack Bruce. Marshall played briefly on *Songs For A Tailor* (1969) but more prominently throughout *Harmony Row* (1971). In the same year, he teamed up with Graham Bond, Chris Spedding and Art Theman in Bruce's excellent but short-lived touring band.

Their debut was a headliner in Hyde Park, supported by King Crimson and Roy Harper and the band, just called Jack Bruce and Friends, blew a storm, playing much of the *Harmony Row* album in the set. Whether playing arrangements or improvisations, they were tight and exhilarating on stage. Marshall who operates primarily on the jazz scene, has appeared on the following: *Songs For A Tailor* (1969) & *Harmony Row* (1971) by Jack Bruce, *Solar Plexus* Ian Carr's Nucleus (1971), *Fifth* (1972)

Sixth (1973) *Seventh* (1974) *Softs* (1976) *Alive and Well In Paris* (1978) & *Land Of Cockayne* (1981) all by Soft Machine.

Harvey Mason

A well-schooled ace Los Angeles funk drummer with enormous experience gained from doing everything from strip clubs to opera, from George Benson sessions to BENSON the T.V. show. When he first moved from Atlantic City, where he grew up, to Los Angeles, it was his percussion work that was in demand, rather than his drumming, but once he got a break on the Sammy Davis show, people started taking notice of Harvey Mason 'The Drummer'. During the seventies, he started releasing solo albums and producing other artists like Lee Ritenour. He recently made an unusual move for an American drummer, by switching to drums made by the British Premier Drum Company, being particularly impressed with their comprehensive range of percussion.

On record
His solo albums are okay, but tend towards the over-slick and glossy. The best two to date are *Earthmove* (1976) and *Funk In A Mason Jar* (1977). His addition of vocals on this album (his own, incidentally), pushed up sales five-fold on previous efforts.

Also: *In Flight* (1977) & *Breezin'* (1976) by George Benson, *I Wanna Play For You* Stanley Clarke (1979), *Headhunters* Herbie Hancock (1973 – probably the most significant album Mason has worked on as it heralded Hancock's move away from jazz to more commercial work. Virtually the whole album is based on rhythmic riffs. The opening track *Chameleon* typified the new Hancock approach to his music), *Swing of Delight* Carlos Santana (1980), *It Looks Like Snow* Phoebe Snow (1976), *Secrets* Gil Scott Heron (1978).

Nick Mason

Nick Mason has been associated with Pink Floyd comrades Rick Wright and Rogers Waters since their days together at Regent Street Polytechnic and a band called Sigma 6 which became T Set (with Syd Barrett), the Screaming Abdabs and finally the Abdabs playing R&B. A blues duo named Pink Anderson and Floyd Council inspired a name change to

the Pink Floyd Sound, but once the last word was dropped, the sound moved far away from the cotton fields of Mississippi or the Chicago ghetto into outer space and the universe of cosmic rock.

As a drummer, Nick Mason has always been fairly unpretentious and straightforward for some years now, even discarding his one piece of personal spectacular when the gong would burst into flames during *Set The Controls For The Heart Of The Sun*. Over the years he has remained content just to lay down some earthy rhythms, largely consisting of rolls around the kit with his trusty felt beaters, faster or slower as the song dictated. Neither does he seem that bothered about drums as an instrument, preferring to concentrate on the studio high technology of production; in a recent interview, he didn't even know what size his Ludwig bass drums were. Willie Wilson is used as a second drummer on stage.

Nevertheless, Mason's simplicity has always been an asset to Pink Floyd, helping to hold the sound together, especially important during long improvisational pieces and acting as a reference point for the rest of the band on stage. Certainly their earlier work such as *Piper At The Gates Of Dawn* (1967), *A Saucerful Of Secrets* (1968) and *Ummagumma* (1969) would not have sounded the same without him. Recently he released an interesting solo album, *Fictitious Sports,* boasting the talents of Carla Bley and Robert Wyatt.

Dave Mattacks

Dave Mattacks is one of Britain's most respected and talented session drummers, combining his studio work with a long history of touring primarily on the folk/rock scene, stretching back to his days with Fairport Convention.

He joined Fairport in 1969 after the death of Martin Lamble, with four years dance band experience to his credit. He came straight in to play on Fairport's masterpiece *Liege and Lief* (1969), although he says he hadn't got his timing completely together on that album which didn't come right in his estimation until the next album *Full House* (1970).

However, by 1972 Mattacks was feeling crowded in by the structure of a working band and, preferring the freedom of the studio where he had already done some session work, he quit Fairport but returned shortly after for another period until 1974. He stayed on the folk/rock scene for outings with the various combinations of musicians who were constantly forming and re-forming bands within this area for one-off gigs, albums or longer, but still adhoc associations such as the Albion Country Band, the Etchingham Steam Band and the Albion Dance Band and he took part in Fairport Convention reunion events. During an interview he gave in 1975, he said there were only two bands he would work for, Weather Report ('and I'm not good enough for them') and Stevie Winwood . . . 'and I'd drop everything for Richard Thompson' – for some while, Dave Mattacks has been Richard and Linda Thompson's regular recording and touring drummer.

A musician of consumate skill and grace, his many recordings include Liege and Lief *(1969) &* Full House *(1970) by Fairport Convention,* Joan Armatrading *(1976),* Like An Old Fashioned Waltz *(1973) &* Rendezvous *(1977) by Sandy Denny,* Dancer With Bruised Knees *Kate and Anna McGarrigle (1977),* Streets Of London *Ralph McTell (1975),* Pour Down Like Silver *(1975)* First Light *(1978)* Sunny Vista *(1979) &* Shoot Out The Lights *(1982) all by Richard and Linda Thompson.*

Also sessions with Brian Eno, Andy Fairweather Low, Chris Spedding, Russ Ballard, Kiki Dee, Kilburn and the High Roads and Peter Green.

Andrew McCulloch

After stints with Fields and Kingdom Come, Andrew McCulloch replaced Mike Giles in King Crimson for the *Lizards* album (1971) but left almost as soon as it was finished.

He joined Greenslade in 1972 with former Colosseum members Dave Greenslade (keyboards), Tony Reeves (bass) and Dave Lawson (keyboards). A talented drummer, McCulloch was well suited to this technically accomplished band which created complex, stylish arrangements from a stimulating amalgam of jazz, rock and classical influences. Management problems were apparently at the root of their break-up in 1976 and a very disillusioned McCulloch concentrated his efforts in establishing a flight case business.

John Marshall

On record

Spread across their four albums, Greenslade produced some fine music *Greenslade* (1973), *Bedside Manners Are Extra* (1973), *Spyglass Guest* (1974) and *Time and Tide* (1975) – some of the playing times, however, were not over-generous.

Ralph McDonald

Reckoned to be the world's best percussionist, he joined Harry Belafonte in 1958, when he was still a teenager and stayed with him for ten years, moving on to play with Roberta Flack for another five. In 1975, he set up Antisia music with bassist William Sulter and started producing in the Antisia-owned studios Rosebud. He was one of the first percussionists to use the percussion synthesiser known as a syndrome. Apart from his numerous session outings, McDonald has released some very fine solo albums, *Sound Of A Drum* (1976), *The Path* (1978) and *Counterpoint* (1979). *The Path* shows off very imaginative use of synthesised percussion, light years beyond the normal way such technology is handled, i.e. boring to the point of instant cliché. Studio musicians who appear on these albums include Grosvenor Washington, Richard Tee, Eric Gale, Rick Marotta, Chuck Rainey, Randy Brecker, Steve Gadd, Tom Scott and Bob James.

On record

McDonald sessions include: *Come As You Are* (1976) & *Is It Still Good To You* (1978) by Ashford & Simpson, *Average White Band* (1974), *Queen Of The Night* Maggie Bell (1973), *Breezin'* George Benson (1976), *Young Americans* David Bowie

Buddy Miles

(1975), *The Brecker Brothers* (1975), *Watermark* Art Garfunkel (1977), *Abandoned Luncheonette* Hall & Oates (1973), *Garland Jeffreys* (1973), *52nd Street* Billy Joel (1978), *Thoroughbred* Carole King (1976), *Sweet Revenge* John Prine (1974), *Street Lights* Bonnie Raitt (1974), *One Trick Pony* Paul Simon (1980), *Gaucho* Steely Dan (1980).

Robbie McIntosh

Original member of the Average White Band, a superb funk drummer whose hard, tight sound was the in-

spiration behind the closest Britain ever came to having a true soul band. Their excellent second album *AWB* (1974) really set them up in America in a big way and then tragedy struck – McIntosh overdosed on heroin, thinking it to be cocaine. A year later, a court believed it was no accident but murder. Ex-Brian Auger drummer, Steve Ferrone eventually replaced McIntosh but though more than competent, he did not have McIntosh's extra sparkle and dynamism. *AWB* was their finest hour, but the debut album *Show Your Hand* (1973) was also impressive.

Ted McKenna

During the early months of 1972, after eight years as leader of the Alex Harvey Soul Band and four years in the show group of the rock musical Hair, Alex Harvey decided he wanted to get back on the road. In Glasgow he discovered a powerful rock band called Teargas, who had made two poor selling albums – the band were Zal Cleminson (guitar) Chris Glen (bass), Hugh McKenna (keyboards) and Ted on drums. Harvey and Teargas got together and the result was a glorious rock theatre creation – The Sensational Alex Harvey Band. The live act was truly sensational – Ted McKenna

driving the band relentlessly and skilfully through Harvey's vignettes, introducing characters like the Tomahawk Kid and Vambo played out with panache and style against this hard rock backdrop. Amid acrimony and Harvey's bad health, the band broke up after six years; Harvey himself was then very quiet making occasional appearances before his untimely death in 1982 after a heart attack. The band carried on briefly and unsuccessfully as SAHB without Alex, then split up completely, McKenna going on to play with Rory Gallagher on *Photo Finish* (1978) and *Top Priority* (1979). Towards the end of the SAHB saga, keyboardist Tommy Eyre came in for Hugh McKenna;

Ted McKenna and Eyre resumed their working relationship in the recently formed Greg Lake band. The 1981 Lake tour had McKenna performing as impressively as ever behind his Premier kit.

On record

McKenna was always very visible on SAHB albums, particularly on *SAHB Live* (1975) and the spine-chilling *Faith Healer* and a later, undeservedly neglected SAHB album *Rockdrill* (1978).

Buddy Miles

A powerful but technically limited drummer, Buddy Miles was playing professionally at 15 with the Inkspots and later in Wilson Pickett's band and at that time he was a good soul drummer. Then in 1967 he teamed up with the late Mike Bloomfield to form Electric Flag, an early 'supergroup' boasting Barry Goldberg, Nick Gravenites and Harvey Brooks. But despite a successful debut appearance at the 1967 Monterey Festival, their career together was short, destroyed by the pressures that combined virtuosity can cause and the fact that their attempt to create a rock/soul/jazz amalgam was always rather tentative and uneasy. Nevertheless, *A Long Time Comin'* (1968) was a fine album and the best thing Buddy Miles ever did, by a long way. After the Flag broke up, Miles decided to try his hand at band leading and formed the Buddy Miles Express, releasing a reasonable soul-based rock album called *Expressway To Your Skull* (1968). Unfortunately, the album's bludgeoning over-the-top title tended to epitomise Miles' whole approach to his career from here on in. Possibly due to the political pressure on Hendrix to form an all black band, and being one of the few candidates, Buddy Miles found himself in the Band Of Gypsies, an unhappy period in Hendrix's career, which collapsed after one album. Continuing his existence as a band leader, Buddy Miles, now dabbling additionally with guitar, bass and keyboards, went on through the Seventies producing one dire album after another, over a dozen so far, salvaging only one success from the morass, *Them Changes* (1970) whose title track produced a hit single.

In his time, Miles has been involved in some unlikely associations; session drumming on John McLaughlin's *Devotion* album (1971), a hideous

live collaboration with Carlos Santana in 1972 and mutual session appearances with Adrian and Paul Gurvitz; Miles on their *A Third Of A Lifetime* (1971) with Three Man Army and them on his *Chapter VII* (1973).

The American music scene, and in particular the rock critics, seem to regard Buddy Miles as something of a joke, not least because his inordinate appetite for self-publicity has not been backed up by any worthwhile material. It seems that he could not accept that he was just a competent funk drummer – he wanted to be more, but anyone who starts off an interview by saying 'This gun is loaded', is going to have a hard time trying to get people to take them seriously.

Mitch Mitchell

John 'Mitch' Mitchell started doing deputising sessions for Screaming Lord Sutch, Johnny Kid and the Pirates and a host of others while he was still a teenager going through drama school, where incidentally, he did tap dancing à la Steve Gadd and Buddy Rich. Thus he was already an experienced drummer by the time he turned professional with a mid-Sixties R&B band called the Riot Squad. The line-up included Jon Lord and Graham Bonnet and they toured with The Kinks, recorded a string of unsuccessful singles. He had longish stints with the Pretty Things and Georgie Fame before his ultimate experience – Jimi Hendrix.

The musical relationship between Hendrix and Mitchell remains unique in rock – there has never really been such a symbiosis between a rock drummer and the lead instrument, previously seen only in the immortal bonds forged between Elvin Jones and John Coltrane, Tony Williams and Miles Davis.

The rhythmic role assigned to Noel Redding (which in truth he didn't always keep to), allowed Mitchell to explore the wider arena of free form playing, not usually permissible in a heavy rock. But he never forgot the prime task of any drummer, keeping time and anchoring down the sound which he did masterfully with cracking military snare pulses and double time bass drum rolls – sharp, punctuating rhythmic sequences rolling back and forth, running with the tide of Hendrix's peerless guitar playing.

When the show was finally over for Mitch Mitchell, he largely dis-

appeared from view. He surfaced occasionally to record an album with a band called *Ramatan* (1972) and plays gigs with Larry Coryell, Jack Bruce, Terry Reid and more recently, Hinckley's Heroes and Roger Chapman. Under the pseudonym of Henry Manchovitz, he played on Randy California's *Kaptain Kopter* album (1972). Much of his time nowadays is spent doing American TV commercials.

Both Mitch Mitchell and Noel Redding have been keeping a low profile for over a decade – which is a hell of a long time. To some extent it's hardly surprising. Apart from some of the extremely heavy scenes that went down during those days when Hendrix was earning more than anyone else in the history of rock music, when you have done everything, seen everything and above all played with the greatest rock musician there has ever been, and you're still in your early twenties – where else is there to go? It is a shame that Mitchell did become a recluse in this way because, at the beginning of the seventies, jazz/rock or fusion was just start-

ing and, judging by his playing with Hendrix, he could have made a major contribution to that scene, if he could ever have shaken off the mantle of being 'Hendrix's drummer'. Perhaps that was the problem.

And from the 'would you believe it' department: Mitch Mitchell was a child actor in the British TV school comedy series WACKO! with Jimmy Edwards and he was taught jazz licks by the late Peter Sellers, also a drummer in his time.

On record

Musicians on the scene at the time, couldn't believe how far Mitch Mitchell had come as a drummer, from playing with Georgie Fame to Jimi Hendrix. His maturity and confidence were astonishing, drumming of the highest calibre marking him out as one of the greats. The first four Hendrix albums are the indispensable legacies of his greatness, Mitchell playing superbly well throughout especially on: *Fire, Can You See Me, Manic Depression, Smash Hits* (1967), *3rd Stone From The Sun, Are You Experienced* (1967), *Spanish Castle Magic, Axis: Bold As Love* (1967),

Voodoo Chile, Crosstown Traffic, Electric Ladyland (1968).

Ziggy Modeliste

One of New Orleans' finest drummers and as drummer with the Meters, possibly *the* funk percussionist of modern times.

Originally Fats Doimino's backing band, they were the Hawkettes and the Neville Sound, before changing their name after doing some sessions for Allen Toussaint. The Meters are Cyril Neville (percussion), Art Neville (keyboards), Leo Nocentilli (guitar) George Parker (bass) and Joseph 'Ziggy' Modeliste who is also a master percussionist on congas and bongos. Studio session musicians at Seascent Studios, they specialise in clipped off beat accents and rhythms based on Modeliste's impeccable time-keeping. Even when playing intricate percussion patterns, he never wavers a fraction. They have played on Lee Dorsey, Betty Harris and Dr.

John hits, worked with Paul McCartney, Jess Roden and Robert Palmer and toured with the Rolling Stones in 1975. Modeliste played drums on the New Barbarians tour.

On record

The Meter's own music of the Sixties can be regarded as the forerunner of much seventies funk, in particular singles like *Sophisticated Cissy* (1968). They signed to Warner Brothers in an attempt to widen their audience and of the four albums recorded, *Rejuvenation* (1974) emerged as their finest music ever – modern New Orleans funk at its most exhilarating.

Pierre Moerlen

One of the finest drummers Europe has ever produced, French born Moerlen has had an in and out relationship with Gong since 1973, although more recently he has emerged as the band's leader. Moerlen learned his enormous skills at the Strasbourg Conservatory and became well versed in all types of tuned percussion as well as drums, excelling particularly on vibes. On stage, Moerlen and fellow percussionist Francois Causse, switch effortlessly from delicate tuned percussion interplay on vibes or marimbas to thunderous rhythmic cross patterns on Gretsch and Ludwig drums. Very much neglected and deserving of far more international recognition, Moerlen is stunning on the following Gong albums, *Gazeuse* (1977), *Live* (1977), *Time Is The Key* (1979) and *Pierre Moerlen's Gong Live* (1979).

Keith Moon

It is a great shame that due to the scurrilous gutter press, the legacy of Keith Moon in most people's minds is of a string of broken hotel rooms, rather than that of a very skilful, demonic drummer whose ferocious, abandoned style helped make the Who the greatest rock band in the world.

Born in 1947, Moon's early stamping ground was Wembley in North London; Charlie Watts and Ginger Baker lived nearby. As a sixteen year old £6 a week plasterer's mate, he would deputise in any band that would have him. Drum entrepreneur Gerry Evans played in a group called the Men Of Mystery, whose gimmick was to wear masks. Moon 'depped'

for him once – and only once. Next morning, the lads came round to Evans' house demanding an explanation. Wearing his £21 gold lamé suit which was totally outrageous for 1962 and which he insisted on wearing everywhere (even to the chip shop), Keith Moon had smashed the drum kit to bits. And he hadn't even joined the Who yet!

When he did – the visual and aural impact was overwhelming – he seemed to be playing all the drums, all at once, a tumultuous, cascading tightly tuned onslaught, but all tied into a concept of unpredictable playing. Tom-tom rolls didn't have to end in a cymbal crash, fill-ins were played in the same metre so there was no let up in the pace, and overall the drums were often moved into the front line as a lead instrument, Moon at times, eschewing the restrictions imposed upon the drummer as time-keeper, relinquishing the job to John Entwhistle. With such a full and expansive approach, Moon had no use for solos and never played them. Moon's first kit was a £120 Premier bought in 1961 and he stayed loyal to the company from then on, pioneering the large kit by adding more and more to the basic (!) double kick-drum seven piece that he first had with the Who. Ginger Baker started using a double Ludwig around the same time. One of Moon's most famous set-ups was his custom-built *Pictures Of Lily* kit commissioned from Premier in the late Sixties – each drum panel containing pictures of said Lily in a variety of interesting positions; the masturbatory fantasy woman of the song came to life. Moon's kit grew and grew, some of the tom-toms hardly within striking distance. Each drum had to be set at the correct angle and tuned tight, not slack as is usual in rock. A roadie's life is not a happy one.

Keith Moon died of a drug overdose in 1978, in the same flat in which Mama Cass Elliott passed away four years ealier – but forget the Muppet image, the explosions, the booze, the mania – that was not really Keith Moon enjoying himself. He got his biggest kicks out of driving the Who and the safest place for him to be was on the stage doing what he did best – listen to *The Who Live At Leeds* (1970) and hear Keith Moon – the drummer.

Airto Moreira

Winner of countless music polls as the world's No. 1 percussionist (including

the *Downbeat* poll six years on the trot), Airto Moreira came to the States from Brazil in the late Sixties. After ten years club and cabaret experience in Sao Paulo and Rio De Janeiro, he started recording with Miles Davies and Chick Corea, indicating the strength of his reputation even then. As well as numerous sessions, Airto is a considerable writing talent, with over half a dozen albums to his credit, supported by such luminaries as Keith Jarrett, Stanley Clarke, Ron Carter and Chick Corea. Airto is a phenomenal percussionist and drummer and his large and varied catalogue includes: *Feel No Fret* Average White Band (1979), *Return To Forever* (1972) & *Live in New York '74* (1975) by Chick Corea, *My Goal's Beyond* John McLaughlin (1971), *Don Juan's Reckless Daughter* Joni Mitchell (1977), *Borboletta* Santana (1974), *There Goes Rhymin' Simon* Paul Simon (1973), *Awakening* Narada Michael Walden (1979), *Weather Report* (1970).

Of his solo albums, the best are *Fingers* (1973), *Free* (1975) and *The Essential Airto* (1977). He has also been involved with Grateful Dead drummers, Bill Kreutzman and Micky Hart in their band the Rhythm Devils and plays on the album *Play River Music* (1980); Brazilian percussion featured in the sound track of APOCALYPSE NOW executed by Kreutzman and Hart.

Barry Morgan

British session musician who was associated with the hit single session group Blue Mink with Madeline Bell, Roger Cooke and Herbie Flowers, now of Sky. Morgan's rock sessions have included: *Rainmaker* (1969) Michael Chapman, *I've Got The Music In Me* (1974) Kiki Dee, *Right Now* (1979) Georgie Fame, *That's What Friends Are For* (1979) Georgie Fame, *Time and Tide* (1975) Greenslade, *Elton John* (1970), *Madman Across The Water* (1971), *Izitso* (1977) Cat Stevens, *Chris Spedding* (1976).

Rod Morganstein

Ace drummer with the Dregs (formerly the Dixie Dregs) who, after five years slog, are gradually gaining the recognition they deserve in the States although they are virtually un-

known in Britain apart from one track, *Take It Off The Top,* used by disc jockey Tommy Vance as the theme music for his radio show.

Although the whole band is greatly influenced by the Mahavishnu Orchestra, the Dregs is a very eclectic bunch with a repertoire ranging from fusion and orchestral rock to Allman boogie music and the country sounds of the Burrito Brothers – all on the same album! This eclectism proved problematical from a marketing point of view, part of the reason for their slow climb up the ladder. Fortunately, the band were not tempted into a musical compromise and carried on regardless, until the American public finally picked up on what they had been missing and fortunes changed for the better. Such is their reputation, that at a recent Los Angeles gig, Jaco Pastorius brought a few friends along to see them – Lenny White, Michael Walden, McLaughlin, Beck and Stanley Clarke.

Rod Morganstein therefore has to play across the whole spectrum of modern rock music and his great versatility is matched only by the ease and power of his execution. His drumming is very "musical" or lyrical, a reflection of his formal music training on piano as well as percussion, such that he had a difficult choice as to what his main instrument was going to be. He breezed through his audition with the prestigious New York Jazz Band before moving south to Miami where he met up with Steve Morse, the Dregs' lead guitarist and main creative inspiration.

Morganstein is not only a visual and energetic drummer on stage, but also in the studio, prone to grunting right through a session, as he drives the band through their often furious paces. Unfortunately, the studio mikes were picking up these exclamations of effort, so he played through the whole of one album session with his mouth taped up! Morganstein plays Rogers drums.

On record
The Dregs have recorded five albums to date. *What If* (1978) being the best so far: *Freefall* (1977), *What If* (1978) (including *Take It Off The Top*), *Night Of The Living Dregs* (1979), *Unsung Heroes* (1980), *Crank It Up* (1982) (at the time of writing it is unavailable in the UK – Morganstein shines on this one).

For all you musos who thought virtuoso rock music was dead – fear not –

Barry Morgan

the Dregs are at hand. Do Yourself a favour and listen to the band who will hopefully become BIG NEWS.

Ian Moseley

Talented young British musician on Tama drums, who started out as a drum salesman in the famous West End drum store Drum City, run by the equally famous Gerry Evans.

Moseley's sessions have included the pop band Fox, fronted by French vocalist Noosha Fox and *Peacock Party* Gordon Giltrap (1980), *Night Music* (1974), *Wolf* (1974) and *Converto* (1978) all by Darryl Way.

Moseley also featured in a band called Trace with Darryl Way again. He replaced former Focus drummer Pierre Van Der Linden and played on *Birds* (1975).

Alphonse Mouzon

Born in Charleston, South Carolina in 1948, Alphonse Mouzon moved to New York in 1966, ostensibly to study medicine, but ending up playing in the Ross Carnegie Orchestra before turning freelance with artists like Gil Evans, Tim Hardin, Chubby Checker (!) and Roberta Flack. He was Weather Report's first drummer in 1970, played with McCoy Tyner in 1972, Larry Coryell's Eleventh House from 1973-74, when he went solo. He was back with Coryell from 1976-77 but since 1978 has been a solo recording artist. During the Seventies he had also worked with Eric Clapton, Stevie Wonder, Al Dimeola and Patrick Moraz.

It was during his first period with Larry Coryell that he first came to public attention as a blisteringly fast and versatile power-house fusion drummer from the Cobham school, who made most other drummers sound like they were asleep. Dressed up to the nines (no Cobham T-shirt and trainers for this cat – he played in stack heels!), he would tear into his kit like a man possessed. To accomplish the superbly controlled rippling snare patterns, gale-force cymbal thrashing and dazzling tom-tom/bass drum rolls, he would often have to stand up to get right round the kit. Has played Fibes, Pearl and Sonor kits.

On record
His early solo albums were patchy affairs, uneasy mixes of funk, rock and

fusion, although *Mind Transplant* (1975) has the talents of Tommy Bolin on guitar and the energetic and torrential Mouzon drum technique is never less than staggering if you accept his tendency to over-play. *The Essence of Mystery* (1975), his first, was the best until *Virtue* (1977), littered with good blowing jazz arrangements, executed by sensitive musicians. The album's *pièce de résistance* is the *Mouzon Drum Suite,* which traces Afro-American history through the drum.

Despite the presence of musicians like Herbie Hancock, Lee Ritenour and Freddie Hubbard, later albums such as *By All Means* (1981) are not totally satisfying.

The two best pieces of playing outside the solo context, are *Weather Report* (1970) and *Introducing Eleventh House* (1974) – Larry Coryell.

Jamie Muir

He came from nowhere and, legend has it, disappeared back there – to a monastery in Cornwall. On his way, around July 1972, this extraordinary musician came into King Crimson and on *Lark's Tongue In Aspic* (1972), the album he named, laid down percussive patterns of breathtaking power and intricacy. It remains Crimson's finest hour. Bill Bruford threw up his very lucrative position in Yes, mainly for the chance of playing with the percussionist, who subsequently exerted a great influence on his playing. The name of Jamie Muir is still spoken of in hushed whispers – the man who made Syd Barrett look like a socialite.

Sandy Nelson

With hit singles like *Teenbeat* (1959) and *Let There Be Drums* (1961) Sandy

Nelson became the first star of rock drumming, bringing the art out of the shadow of jazz percussion and, as the hardware improved, giving it new status and credibility. Rock percussion was given a similar impetus by Hal Blaine and his work on Phil Spector hits.

Nelson first played with Bruce Johnston of the Beach Boys in an obscure Santa Monica band called Kip Tyler and the Flips and toured with the Teddy Bears, playing on their massive hit *To Know Him Is To Love Him* in 1958. He moved into session work prior to recording his own hit singles, playing on Gene Vincent's *Crazy Times* album (1959). Just before becoming a big star, Nelson actually had his left foot amputated after a car crash.

Many a big name rock drummer started out by thumping away to Sandy Nelson records in the back bedroom while the neighbours banged on the walls either side.

Tony Newman

One of the legendary characters of British drumming, Tony Newman and his famous jet black Trixon kit featured in a popular Sixties instrumental group called Sounds Incorporated, who backed American artists on tour in the UK and once signed to Brian Epstein in 1964, found themselves opening for the Beatles at Shea Stadium.

They appeared on the Sgt Pepper album on *Good Morning, Good Morning*. When the group split up around 1968, Tony Newman fittingly joined a band of diamond hard personalities led by Jeff Beck with Rod Stewart, Ron Wood and Nicky Hopkins. With such a fierce chemistry at work, the band not surprisingly broke up with only six months of 1969 gone, but managed to get the thunderous *Beck-Ola* in the can. From there, Newman worked in an undistinguished British rock band called May Blitz before moving on to play with David Bowie, Marc Bolan and Kevin Ayers until 1975, when he formed Boxer with former Patto and Spooky Tooth vocalist, Mike Patto. They were a hard rocking band, adding Tim Boigart to a later line-up but they suffered from a lack of good material and internal hassles.

Their second album *Bloodletting* (1976), was not released and the cover of the first album depicting a montage of a naked woman being punched in the crotch, was banned. Once Boxer fell apart, Newman decided he'd had enough and headed for hard-drinking cowboy country and the session scene of Nashville.

On record

Sounds Incorporated (1964), *Twist At The Star Club Hamburg* (1964) & *Top Gear* (EP – 1964) all by Sounds Incorporated, *Beck-Ola* Jeff Beck (1969), *May Blitz* (1970) & *Second Of May* (1970) by May Blitz, *Headroom* Alan Clarke (Hollies) (1973), *Three Man Army* (1973) & *Three Man Army 2* (1974) by the Gurvitz Brothers, *Play, Don't Worry* Mick Ronson (1975), *Back To The Night* Joan Armatrading (1975), *Below The Belt* Boxer (1975).

Andy Newmark

Inevitably partnered by the incomparable Willie Weeks on bass, Andy Newmark has played his way round the world with everyone from Sly Stone to Patrick Moraz, always with great economy of effort, lots of tasteful understatement, never too obtrusive, never playing through a song, but laying down just enough for the right effect. He can be heard on: *Young Americans* David Bowie (1975), *Twin Sons Of Different Mothers* Dan Fogelberg (1978), *Rickie Lee Jones* (1979), *Wrap Around Joy* Carole King (1974), *Jesus Was A Capricorn* Kris Krisofferson (1973), *I Came To Dance* Nils Lofgren (1977), *I* (1976) & *Out Of The Sun* (1977) by Patrick Moraz, *Kindling* Gene Parsons (1974), *Fresh* Sly Stone (1973), *First Light* Richard and Linda Thompson (1978), *You Can't Argue With A Sick Mind* Joe Walsh (1975), *Stevie Winwood* (1977), *Dream Weaver* Gary Wright (1976); and just about every Carly Simon album; sessions with Rod Stewart, George Harrison and Roy Buchanan.

New Wave

Readers will, I hope, forgive the liberties taken with the term New Wave, in listing the drummers below – it is used here as a 'catch all' phrase to cover the tortuous byways of punk, pop, new romantics, new psychedelia, new boots and panties, etc. Yet despite the wide diversity of styles represented under these monikers, from the Sex Pistols to Ultravox, the approach adopted to percussion is broadly similar – simple hypnotic beat drumming in rebellion against the cult of technique. This comes across most vividly in the early punk style of the late Seventies, where acoustic drumming was an integral part of the whole collective, communistic, maelstrom of brutal uncompromising sound – rasping snares, thudding tom-toms, fractured angular rhythms that drove home the politics of boredom with sledge hammer savagery.

The hardware was a throw-back to the earliest beat group days, often just a basic cheap four-piece, with a cymbal or two – vast kits were out from a practical, musical and philosophical point of view; you can't play *Anarchy In The U.K.* on a triple bass drum Tama. The revolution in electronic percussion saw this principle carried over into the more refined, slick, commercial arena, using all the new technology for the pre-programming and execution of precise, unswerving, metronomic pulses.

The representative selection of drummers listed here are all powerful no-nonsense musicians, not technicians in the accepted sense, and they might even feel insulted if you suggested they were, but exciting and energetic drummers within the minimalist milieu they help to define. The drum sounds obtained on many new wave records are a sheer delight; full, bright and right up in the mix.

Jet Black
Moving on from *Give 'em Enough Rope*, we have the Stranglers. Jet Black has played the rare Promoco black kit – only about four were ever made. During an interview with *Melody Maker,* he said 'You're going to ask me what my influences are, and my only influence is alcohol. That drove me on.' *Rattus Norvegicus* (1977), *No More Heroes* (1978).

Rick Buckler
Thunderous anchor man with the Jam. Buckler carries the responsibilities of being the drummer in a three-piece band with great gusto and precision. *All Mod-Cons* (1978), *In The City* (1977) and *This Is The Modern World* (1977), give some idea of what Keith Moon might have sounded like on a small drum kit. Plays Premier drums.

Jet Black

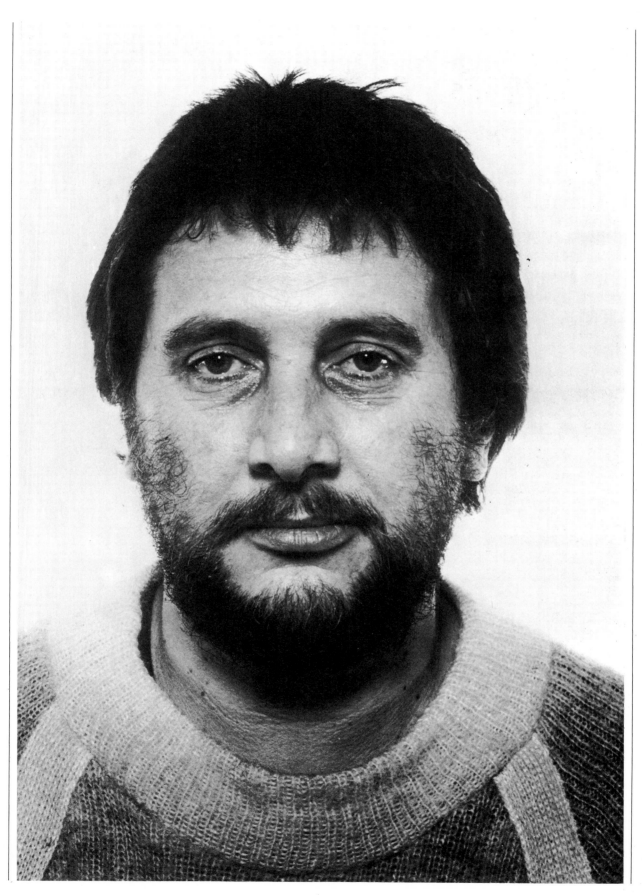

Martin Chambers

Rat Scabies

Budgie

A Pearl drummer who moved from Big In Japan to the Spitfire Boys, then the Slits (unable to find a competent female drummer) and finally Siouxsie and the Banshees (whose very first drummer was none other than Sid Vicious). Budgie replaced the equally effective Kenny Morris. *Kaleidoscope* (1980) – hypnotic and compulsive.

Clem Burke

Previously in Sweet Revenge, a New Jersey rock band and currently with Blondie, whom he joined late in 1974. Using a Premier Resonator kit, pumping out a big boomy sound, Burke generates much of the excitement of Blondie on stage with his exuberant style of playing. *Eat To The Beat* (1979).

Warren Cann

Original member of Ultravox when Denis Leigh né John Foxx was still their frontman back in '74. An early experimenter with electronic percussion, he is outstanding on *Vienna* (1981).

Martin Chambers

Highly competent stixman with the Pretenders – he has to be with time signatures like 27/4 (*The Phone Call*) and 15/4 (*Tattooed Love Boys*) to cope with the tempo on *Bad Boys Get Spanked* is hardly a cakewalk either. Interesting 'reverse-rock' approach to drumming adopted on occasion by Stewart Copeland among others in the aftermath of the disco and punk explosions, whereby the bass drum hits every beat while the rest of the kit is used mainly for accents.

Paul Cook

One of the top half dozen pioneers of the New Wave and the best drummer of the lot. Ever present member of the Sex Pistols, whose importance in the

history of the British music scene fair boggles the mind. Also hung around with the likes of Phil Lynott in the Greedy Bastards, playing a few *ad hoc* gigs. Cook and Jones went on to form the Professionals, who not long after the release of their album *I Didn't See It Coming* (1981), were involved in an horrendous road crash in America. All are on the mend, but it was bloody close. Needless to say *the* album to hear is *Never Mind The Bollocks* (1977).

Pete De Freitas

Industrious and meticulous drummer with Echo And the Bunnymen – his high definition drumming well to the fore on *Crocodiles* (1980).

Nick 'Topper' Headon

Prior to joining The Clash, Topper Headon was a soul band drummer on the U.K. Airforce base circuit in Germany. Produced by Blue Oyster Cult producer Sandy Pearlman, *Give 'Em Enough Rope* (1978) has some dynamic punk drumming on display, exemplified by the snare intro to *Safe European Homes*. A Pearl drummer, who recently announced his departure from the Clash due to, yes you've guessed it, 'musical differences'.

Mark Laff

Subway sect, Generation X plus work with Bernie Torme. *Generation X* (1978), *Valley Of Dolls* (1979). Damn fine drummer as these albums demonstrate.

Steve Nicol

Powerhouse drummer with Eddie and the Hot Rods. *Life On The Line* (1977), particularly *Do Anything You Wanna Do*.

Steve Parry

Canadian drummer who came into the Radio Stars replacing Jim Toomey, himself a replacement for the excellent Chris Townson, who managed to break a leg playing football. Parry was recently invited to join Billy Cobham for a drum clinic shown on British television. *Song For Swinging Lovers* (1977).

Tommy Ramone

Originally manager, then drummer in the Ramones playing high speed frantic percussion in one tempo. If the New York marathon were run on hands rather than feet, he'd be in with a great chance. Quit the road to become a producer and was replaced by Marc Bell, ex-Dust, Wayne County and Richard Hell. *Ramones* (1976) says all there is to say, really. Utterly unique.

Rat Scabies

Another very proficient drummer, who apart from playing with the Damned, has been forming and busting up bands since 1978, like there was no tomorrow: the Vicious White Kids with dear Sid, the White Cats, Doomed and King to name but four. Pre-Damned bands included Rot and the Subterraneans. Plays Pearl drums. *Damned, Damned, Damned* (1977) was the first punk album.

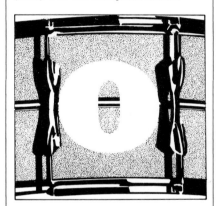

Jamie Oldaker

Tulsa born and bred, Jamie Oldaker, Eric Clapton's drummer from 1974-1978, had his first big break with Bob Seger and the Borneo Band. They cut *Back in '72*, Seger's best album but, amazingly, it is still deleted despite Seger's subsequent success. After the Seger band, Oldaker played around Tulsa clubs with J. J. Cale until he joined Shelter Records as a house drummer, doing sessions and gigs with Leon Russell. Carl Radle was also in the Shelter touring band; he was in touch with Clapton, sent him some tapes and when the band was fired, Radle and Oldaker found themselves in the 1974 Clapton tour and laying down tracks for the classic *461 Ocean Boulevard*. Oldaker plays superbly on this album – his time keeping and fills are spot on and equal to all the demands made of him on tracks like *Motherless Children* and *I Shot The Sheriff*. Similarly, *Backless,* with its leanings towards country music.

When he left Clapton, Oldaker had two stints with Peter Frampton in 1979 and 1981 as the guitarist tried to pick up the pieces of his career and in between he had some gruelling session experience with the Bee Gees in their Middle Ear studio. His time keeping was checked stroke for stroke against a drum machine and each section of the kit was recorded separately on a different track – bass, snare, hihat, etc. Not guaranteed to put a drummer at his ease!

Nowadays, Oldaker is involved in a studio enterprise and plays in a band called Life with George Terry, various ex-Bee Gee sidemen and bassist Howard Coward, formerly John Fred of John Fred and the Playboy Band (*Judy in Disguise*). Jamie Oldaker has been playing Yamaha drums for some years.

On record

461 Ocean Boulevard (1974), *There's One In Every Crowd* (1974), *E.C. Was Here* (1975), *Slowhand* (1977) & *Backless* (1978) all by Eric Clapton, *Burglar* (1974) and Freddie King *1934-1976* (1976).

Nigel Olsson

Nigel Olsson and Tony 'Dee' Murray provided the rhythm section for Plastic Penny who had a top ten single hit in 1968 with *Everything I Am*. Both musicians moved on to the last permutation of the Spencer Davis Group before SD packed it in and moved to California. Olsson and Murray parted company briefly when the drummer had a three month stint with Uriah Heep during their formative days in early 1970 when they were having trouble finding a regular drummer but they came together again in the Elton John band later that year. This very successful association lasted until just before Elton John's big Wembley Stadium gig in June 1975 when he decided it was time for a change.

Olsson has done numerous sessions, including the sound track of TOMMY, Bob Weir, Jimmy Webb, Leon Rusell, Rod Stewart, Kiki Dee and Neil Sedaka, as well as some none too successful over-produced solo albums, although he has got a good voice.

A respected and competent, if not outstanding drummer, with a good full and open sound, his recorded work includes: *Empty Sky* (1969), *Tumbleweed Connection* (1970), *Madman Across The Water* (1971), *Honky Chateau* (1972), *Don't Shoot Me* (1973), *Yellow Brick Road* (1973), *Caribou* (1974) & *Captain Fantastic* (1974) all by Elton John, *Boats Against*

Warren Cann

The Current (1977) & *Change Of Heart* (1978) by Eric Carmen, *The Cate Brothers* (1975), *Prisoner In Disguise* Linda Ronstadt (1975), *Very 'umble Very 'eavy* Uriah Heep (1970), *Resurrection* The Big Three (1974 – the revival album of a very popular and highly respected Merseyside Trio, who lay claim to being one of Liverpool's first Sixties beat groups and one of Britain's first three-piece groups).

Ian Paice

Based on his work with Deep Purple, Ian Paice has been a heavy rock drummer of seminal importance, currently undergoing a gratifying renaissance in Whitesnake, demonstrating his immense talents to a whole new audience.

Like John Bonham, Ian Paice has never used a double bass drum kit and is a classic example in heavy rock of how effective the drummer can be who knows when to leave things out – too many just overplay the whole time – and Paice remains a drummer who has exerted singular influence on the new breed of musclemen.

Paice was born in West London and worked as a civil servant while playing in semi-pro bands like George and the Rave Ons until he turned professional with M15, who toured extensively in Europe. Deep Purple's original vocalist, Rod Evans, fronted the band, who changed their name to Maze but broke up when Paice and Evans joined Purple in March 1968. Around this time Paice did some recording with a mysterious band called Green Bullfrog with the amazing line-up of Paice, Ritchie Blackmore, Roger Glover, Albert Lee, Big Jim Sullivan and Jon Lord.

Deep Purple, of course, went on to massive fame, fortune and glory the world over, driven through their paces by one of rock's few bespectacled drummers who remained loyal to his Ludwig kit throughout. The Purple juggernaut finally ground to a halt early in 1976 – Jon Lord and Ian Paice together with keyboardist Tony Ashton laid plans for what proved to be an abortive supergroup called Paice Ashton and Lord, which lasted one album and about twelve months during 1977. Apart from occasional appearances, Ian Paice then dropped out of the public eye altogether, until a call came from David Coverdale and he replaced David Dowle in Whitesnake.

On record
Ian Paice appears on all Deep Purple albums but particularly recommended are *Deep Purple In Rock* (1970), *Made In Japan* (1972) and *Burn* (1974).

Paice has always displayed great snap and sharpness on cymbals, snare and hi-hat, not usual in heavy rock, where tom tom and bass drum work often predominates. This aptitude carried on into his work with Whitesnake and he is in top form particularly on *Ready And Willin'* (1980).

Carl Palmer

A superlative percussionist whose speed, invention and dexterity with Emerson, Lake and Palmer put him in the front rank of world drumming.

As a teenager, he had a short spell at Birmingham School of Music, leaving after only a year because 'they were a load of idiots. I thought I could do just as well myself.' At 15 he was in Chris Farlowe's Thunderbirds, King Bees (recording *Wild Thing* and *Can't Let Go*) and a mid-Sixties Birmingham-based band called Locomotive with Chris Woods of Traffic. At 18 he replaced Drachen Theaker in the Crazy World Of Arthur Brown. Brown was a totally unforgettable loon, doyen of the London underground circuit and expert at setting light to himself, from which sprang his classic No. 1 hit single of August 1968, *Fire*. But very much a novelty, he failed to make any headway after his initial impact and Carl Palmer left in 1969 to form Atomic Rooster with Vincent Crane.

He was with Crane for about a year and then came the Isle of Wight Festival 1970 and the apocalyptic debut of Emerson, Lake and Palmer (once touted as Emerson, Lake, Hendrix and Mitchell). Criticised for being cold and emotionless, ELP were nevertheless a power combination unsurpassed in technical ability, stage dynamics and showmanship.

Carl Palmer's kit was monstrous – later on in his ELP career, he had 2½ tons of stainless steel drums, copper rimmed and engraved with baroque hunting scenes. Each drum had its own synthesiser, synchronised together, plus chimes, tympani, dragon emblazoned gongs and a 134-lb. church bell, all set up on a solid iron riser. ELP blew out one gig in Canada, because the stage couldn't take the weight. Next to this lot, Greg Lake's £2000 Persian carpet on which he stood, seemed a humble trinket.

Unlike many drummers when they attain fame and fortune, Palmer never stopped learning his craft, taking percussion instruction from James Blades at The Royal Academy of Music, further extending his talents to the whole range of tuned percussion.

After ELP came to a slow, messy finish, Palmer tried his hand at band leading with PM, sporting a whole group of unknowns which sank without trace. Back to playing Premier drums after a long period with Gretsch, Palmer is in the money again with Asia (Steve Howe, John Wetton, Geoff Downes), the apothesis of corporate rock who seem set to 'out-Foreigner' everything in sight. The way its been going since the release of their debut album this year, Asia could well be a nuclear power before much longer, but whether Palmer will have quite the same freedom to display his virtuosity is doubtful.

On record
ELP (1970) and *Brain Salad Surgery* (1973) are Palmer's best statements. His drumming on the debut album can only be described as frightening.

Earl Palmer

A big name New Orleans percussionist who played on many Fats Domino records in the fifties, and now a major Hollywood session drummer, B. B. King, Phil Everly, Larry Williams being among his recording credits. Also: *Sweet Harmony* Maria Muldaur (1976), *Look At The Fool* Tim Buckley (1974), *Down On The Farm* Little Feat (1979), *Mary C. Brown* Dory Previn (1972), *Takin' My Time* Bonnie Raitt (1973), *Blue Valentine* Tom Waits (1978), *Sail Away* Randy Newman (1972).

Ian Paice

Ric Parnell

Son of band leader Jack Parnell, he followed Carl Palmer and Paul Hammond in Atomic Rooster, playing well on two otherwise average British rock albums of the early seventies, *Made In England* (1972) and *Nice And Greasy* (1973). He did a session for a band called Nova, *Blink* (1976), which on a later album boasted Michael Walden and Phil Collins, and joined the prestigous Las Vegas circuit as sometime drummer with Tom Jones.

Gene Parsons

Country rock drummer with a good sense of pacing who, with guitarist Clarence White, went through minor league country outfits in the early sixties, Castaways, Cajun Gib and Nashville West, before they both joined the Byrds in 1968. The line-up of Parsons, White, Skip Battin and Roger McGuinn actually stayed together, past lunchtime and tea for almost three years, Parsons himself playing on five albums from 1968 to his departure in 1972, including the hit single *Chestnut Mare* (1971). A year after he left, his excellent solo album *Kindling* (1973) was released, simple but effective bluegrass, sung by Parsons who wrote all the material and played almost entirely acoustically with Clarence White and Andy Newman guesting. He became an A&R man with Briar Records and featured in a sorry revival of the Flying Burrito Brothers. 1979 saw the release of another solo album, *Melodies*.

On record

The albums recorded with Gene Parsons show the Byrds through all phases of being good, *Untitled* (1970), bad, *Byrdmaniax* (1971) & *Farther Along* (1972) and indifferent *Dr. Byrd And Mr. Hyde* (1969) & *The Ballad Of Easy Rider* (1970) – but never again to be brilliant. Gene Parsons also plays on: *Flying Again* (1975) Flying Burrito Brothers, *Last Of The Brooklyn Cowboys* (1973) Arlo Guthrie, *Sail Away* (1972) Randy Newman.

Carl Palmer
Previous pages: Don Henley (top left), Paul Cook (bottom left) and Ian Paice Overleaf: Brian Downey

Neil Peart

A tremendously exciting drummer both visually and aurally, Neil Peart of Rush came into the band in 1974 replacing John Rutsey. His arrival

Neil Peart

proved a turning point for the band; not only because of his outstanding skill as a drummer, but also thanks to his penchant for writing conceptually evocative science fiction inspired lyrics. He is heavily influenced by the American right wing writer Ayn Rand, whose highly dubious philosophical constructs involve social Darwinism and Nietzchean supermen written up as science fiction, resulting in pubescent Dan Dare lyrics like –

We are the Priests of the Temples of Syrinx
Our Great Computers fill the Hallowed Halls
We are the Priests of the Temples

of Syrinx
And the Gifts of Life are held within our walls.
From *2112* (1976)

Some journalists actually took such nonsense seriously and heaped scorn on Peart's 'fascist' head. But whatever its political implications, stuff like this made Rush into a top selling band both on record and in concert.

As with much of Rush's music, Peart's drumming with his one handed triple flams and lightning sprints round the kit, is stylishly over the top, executed with great power and panache.

His drum kit too, has an air of the extraterrestrial about it – a mammoth all wood-shelled double bass drum Tama kit with about a dozen tom-toms, gong, tympani and a whole assortment of tuned percussion suspended around him to give a cage-like effect on stage.

On record
Forgetting the daft lyrics and Mickey Mouse vocals, *Moving Pictures* (1981) is a superb example of Peart in full flight.

Morris Pert

Prolific and very accomplished British percussionist who can be heard on: *Moving Home* Rod Argent (1978), *The Dancer* Gary Boyle (1977), *Moroccan Roll* (1977), *Masques* (1978) & *Do They Hurt* (1980) all by Brand X, *Another Time, Another Place* (1974) & *Let's Stick Together* (1976) by Roxy Music, *Peacock Party* Gordon Giltrap (1980), *Pacific Eardrum* (1977), *Small-creeps Day* Mike Rutherford (1980), *Venus De Vinyl* Cherry Vanilla (1979).

Simon Phillips

Since Billy Cobham first burst on to the scene with the Mahavishnu Orchestra in the early seventies, it is doubtful whether any rock drummer has made such an impact in music circles as Simon Phillips. Among those in the know, his name stands alongside that of Steve Gadd as one of the finest contemporary drummers in the business – he really is that good and still only in his mid-twenties. Already a phenomenon when he was nine years old, he was playing in his father's big band at the age of 12, staying with them until he was 16. When Sid Phillips died and the band folded, Simon moved on to the orchestra pit of JESUS CHRIST SUPERSTAR, doing all kinds of session work as well. He joined Dana Gillespie's band in 1974, and Chopyn with guitarist Ray Russell in 1975, sessioning all the while – film music for THE ODESSA FILE and the soundtrack of EVITA – his reputation as the hottest kid in town growing in leaps and bounds. He toured with Jack Bruce, Stanley Clarke and Jeff Beck, indicative of the esteem in which he is held by the world's best and further demonstrated by the discography below. Currently, he is in the Toyah Wilcox band and doing a concert with Al

Overleaf: Simon Kirke and Charlie Watts

Dimeola. His work on Roger Glover-produced albums such as *Sin After Sin* by Judas Priest and Michael Schenker's album of 1980, show the use of the big "live" muffle-free drum sound now a feature of Phillips' studio work, harking back to 1974 and his early sessions with Glover on the *Butterfly Ball* album (1974) where the sound was largely pioneered. Simon Phillips plays Tama drums.

On record

An intelligent, positive musician of great power and versatility, with all the chops in the book, he has the world at his feet at the moment and his recorded output includes the following with * sessions particularly excellent. *There and Back* Jeff Beck (1980), *The Dancer* (1977) & *Electric Glide* (1978) by Gary Boyle, *How's Tricks* Jack Bruce (1977), *Grand Slam* Chopyn (1975), *Whitesnake* (1977), **Rocks, Pebbles and Sand* Stanley Clark (1980), *Ain't Gonna Play No Second Fiddle* Dana Gillespie (1974), *Visionary* (1974) & *Fear Of The Dark* (1978) by Gordon Giltrap, *Butterfly Ball* Roger Glover (1974), *Cactus Choir* Dave Greenslade (1976), *Sin After Sin* Judas Priest (1977), **801 Live* Phil Manzanera

Simon Phillips
Roger Pope

(1976), *Back On The Streets* Gary Moore (1978), *Hair Of The Dog* Nazareth (1975), **Wolf* Trevor Rabin (1981), **Smallcreeps Day* Mike Rutherford (1980), **Empty Glass* Pete Townsend (1980).

Roger Pope

A fiery and dynamic drummer, powerful and stylish, he played in a popular Sixties Southampton R&B

band called the Soul Agents, Rod Stewart's backing band for a while. Three members of this band, Ian Duck, Dave Glover and Pope went to the original Elton John band until 1971, when they got together with another Elton John sideman, ace guitarist Caleb Quaye to form Hookfoot. A very frustrating band this – with such talent at their disposal they ought to have made it but a major problem was poor material, which as much as anything, killed off their chances of success. Pope had a successful stint in the Kiki Dee band during the revival of interest in her career, and in Howard Werth's band, the Moonbeams before rejoining Elton John around 1975. Nowadays, he resides in the States with a band called Troops playing Ludwig drums.

On record

Sessions with Long John Baldry, Kevin Ayers, Mike Hugg, John Kongos and Nilsson, but more importantly: *Empty Sky* (1969), *Tumbleweed Connection* (1970), *Madman Across The Water* (1971 – at this time he was swapping the drum chair with Nigel Olsson), *Rock Of The Westies* (1975 – probably Elton John's best album, and thanks to Pope's drumming, is hard, fast and exciting) & *Blue Moves* (1976) all by Elton John, *Hookfoot* (1971), *Good Times A Comin'* (1972), *Communications* (1973) & *Roaring* (1974) all by Hookfoot, *I've Got The Music In Me* Kiki Dee (1974 – very fine percussion on this album in particular), *King Brilliant* Howard Werth and The Moonbeams (1975).

Jeff Porcaro

Another top flight West coast session drummer who has been playing since he was knee-high to a cymbal stand. At eighteen he was with Sonny and Cher, but through the seventies, he has been most noticed through his work with Steely Dan. Recently, however, he has taken the unusual step of relinquishing much of his studio work to play in Toto, a band of session musicians which includes his brother Steve on keyboards. Unfortunately, as with many bands of this ilk, the music is slick and glossy but not far short of musak. However, this should not detract from the fact that Jeff Porcaro is an absolutely first-rate drummer; anyone who plays regular-

Cozy Powell
Previous pages: Keith Moon, Phil Collins, Carmine Appice and John Bonham

ly with the likes of Fagan and Becker has got to be the cream off the top of the milk. Porcaro plays Ludwig drums and can be heard on: *The Teaser* Tommy Bolin (1975), *The Pretender* Jackson Browne (1976), *Larry Carlton* (1978), *Modern Man* Stanley Clarke (1978), *Rickie Lee Jones* (1979), *Some People Can Do What They Like* Robert Palmer (1976), *Thunder In My Heart* Leo Sayer (1977), *Pretzel Logic* (1974), *Kay Lied* (1975) and *Gaucho* (1980) all by Steely Dan, *Toto* (1978), *Hydra* (1979) and *Turn Back* (1980) by Toto, *Heartbreak Radio* Rita Coolidge (1981).

Oh yes, and he's got eleven drum kits and fifty snare drums stored in a warehouse, for when he feels like a change!

Cozy Powell

A very influential heavy rock drummer and band leader who, over his long professional career stretching back seventeen years, has lined up with the world's best musicians – Ritchie Blackmore, Jeff Beck, Michael Schenker, Jack Bruce, Dave Clempson, the list goes on. Booted out of school as 'a bad lot', he did his dues playing with a local Cirencester band called the Sorcerers on the grinding German club circuit from 1965 to 1968, which deserved some sort of endeavour award. After a brief stint with Casey Jones and the Engineers (who used to boast the services of Eric Clapton), he rejoined the Sorcerers who became Youngblood and then the Ace Kefford Stand after the arrival of the ex-Move bassist. The Stand, a poor man's Cream lasted about a year. Powell was also moving into session work with Tony Joe White among others and doing Micky Most productions during which time he met Jeff Beck and recorded an album of old Motown hits, never released. Bassist Denis Ball, who had been in the original Sorcerers, was joined in the Stand by his brother Dave on guitar and the two brothers continued with Powell in Big Bertha, another shortlived enterprise for which Powell only played a few gigs. Spring 1971 saw Powell finally team up with Jeff Beck in a formally constituted Jeff Beck Group – 'formally' because Powell had been working with Beck for about a year previous, but only on an *ad hoc* basis.

When Beck inevitably broke up the group about fourteen months later, Powell almost joined Johnny Win-

ter, having been accepted into the band but, in the event, was reunited with the Ball brothers in Bedlam with Frank Aiello on vocals (now a bus driver). Lack of financial support knocked this outfit on the head in mid-1973. From Bedlam to Hammer, names epitomising Powell's commitment to hard rocking music. Something of a 'supergroup' – Hammer comprised Don Airey (keyboards), Bernie Marsden (guitar) and Neil Murray (bass) who replaced Clive Chapman. With Hammer, the seemingly impossible happened – Cozy Powell released three singles, all of which charted – *Man in Black* (May 1974) *Na Na Na* (August 1974), but most significantly the drum record, *Dance With The Devil* which reached No. 3 in November 1973. Despite being recorded 'for a laugh', it proved to be as influential a drum record as the Sandy Nelson singles were in the Sixties which Powell himself used to drum along with. *Dance With The Devil* provided the stimulus for many budding young drummers to take up the sticks, including apparently, the son of jazz pianist Stan Tracy.

Playing virtually non-stop for nine years, Cozy Powell decided he'd had enough for a while and became a racing driver for Hitachi for a few months. Just prior to joining Rainbow in 1975, he tried to get a band together to be called Strange Brew, with Dave Clempson and ex-Humble Pie bassist Greg Ridley, but Powell damaged his wrist playing football and grounded the band before it got off the blocks. Ritchie Blackmore had spotted Powell first in Beck days, and it was a testament to Powell's high musical calibre (and emotional resilience) in the face of Blackmore's stringent standards, that, when the drummer left in 1980, he was Blackmore's longest serving sideman.

He moved to the Michael Schenker Group, but not before gathering together Jack Bruce, Dave Clempson, Don Airey and Max Middleton to record *Over The Top* (1979) and play some gigs.

Never one to let the grass grow under his feet, Powell has announced his decision to leave Michael Schenker for another rest period. Ted McKenna has been recording with the band since.

Cozy Powell is a skilful, ferociously punishing drummer, one of the hardest hitters around and one of the best heavy rock exponents of double bass drum technique, honed to a fine

art after years of playing big kits – originally Ludwig and now Yamaha. His name has been proudly emblazoned on the front of his kit, whoever has been the star of the band and he is a very popular drummer among rock fans. A Joe Public drummer once walked into a drum shop, banged £1500 on the counter and said 'I want a Yamaha kit; if it's good enough for Cozy Powell, t's good enough for me.'

On record

Considering his list of playing credentials, Cozy Powell has not been well served on record over the years. Only recently has the production matched the quality of drumming on show, namely, *Over The Top* (1979) and *MSG Live At Budokan* (1982). Of his earlier recordings – *Bedlam* (1973).

Viv Prince

Many other musicians regard drummers as a bunch of total madmen, a real law unto themselves, but it was Viv Prince who wrote the bible of lunacy during his time with the Pretty Things, a British Sixties R&B band who, in any case, made the so-called 'bad' Rolling Stones look like the Partridge Family.

After periods with the Dauphin St. Trad Band and Carter Lewis and the Southerners (with Jimmy Page), he joined the Pretty Things in 1963. The band had been formed by Dick Taylor when he left the Stones to pursue his art studies after they turned professional. Taylor got together with singer Phil May, bassist John Stax and rhythm guitarist Brian Pembleton. The drumming spot was fluid until they signed with Fontana and Viv Prince was drafted in. The band played raw, frantic R&B inspired by Bo Diddley, whose song *Pretty Thing* gave the band its name and had chart successes with *Rosalyn, Don't Bring Me Down* and *Honey I Need*. They should have gone to America but didn't – instead, they went to Australia and, mainly due to Prince, it was a disaster. He was thrown off the plane for being drunk – he quaffed whisky from his boots, while crawling round the stage, which he then set fire to and so it went on, one outrage after another which, even for a band of looners like the Pretties, was all a bit too much. Prince had to go.

After that debacle, he played

stand-in gigs with the Who, didn't quite make the first rehearsal of the Jeff Beck Band but did make it in the Denny Laine String Band. The Bunch Of Fives was another short-lived Prince exercise; they recorded one single in 1966 and broke up.

On record

However transitory, his links with names like The Who and Jeff Beck, suggest the strength of his worth as a drummer – ably demonstrated by the debut *Pretty Things* album (1965) – it was a shame he could never get it together.

Bernard Purdie

Bernard 'Pretty' Purdie – one of the world's best soul/funk drummers and among one of the best timekeepers, clinically metronomic in execution. His successes and achievements are many, and his immodesty about them is legendary – the chauffeur has been known to set up the drums in the studio wearing white gloves and then to surround the kit in placards announcing the genius of the guy. And this in the studio, remember.

His sharp, penetrating sound can be heard on countless soul classics like *Sweet Soul Music, Can I Get A Witness, Respect, Chain Of Fools,* for stars like Aretha Franklin, Arthur Conley, The Isley Brothers and James Brown. He has also been much in demand on the rock and fusion scene; Larry Coryell, Al Kooper, Herbie Mann, Steely Dan and remarkably enough, Jeff Beck, whose band he was in during 1975. He went on to join ex-Beck sideman Bob Tench, Clive Chapman and Max Middleton in Hummingbird, who together with guitarist Bernie Holland recorded three studio albums of scintillating fusion music, Purdie being involved in the latter two, including the pick of the crop, *We Can't Go On Meeting Like This* (1976).

A Sonor drummer, his solo albums are far too bland and uninspired, not a patch on his recorded work for other artists which includes: *Live At Fillmore West* Aretha Franklin (1971), *King Curtis Live At Fillmore West* (1971 – Purdie's best live work), *Abandoned Luncheonette* Hall and Oates (1973), *We Can't Go On Meeting Like This* (1976) & *Diamond Nights* (1977) by Hummingbird, *The Royal Scam* (1976), *Aja* (1977) & *Gaucho* (1980) all by Steely Dan, *Foreigner* Cat Stevens (1973), *Soul Is*

... Pretty Purdie (1972), *Shaft* (1974). Best of a mediocre bunch. Nice drums, shame about the music.

Pip Pyle

Started out in the sixties with Delivery, a Canterbury blues band who changed to more jazzier arrangements in the mould of Caravan and Soft Machine, with Steve Miller on piano and Lol Coxhill on sax. Vocalist Carol Grimes and bassist Roy Babbington joined during 1969 and stayed until the band broke up in 1971.

After a brief association with Daevid Allen and Gong, Pyle reappeared in an *avant garde* rock ensemble with the neat moniker Hatfield and The North (after a signpost on one of the main roads north out of London). H&TN were a fine band who played excellent music outside of the mainstream and thus did not have a cat in hell's chance of commercial success. The inevitable collapse of the band saw Pyle move off into session work but he bounced back in a quasi-resurrection of H&TN containing three ex-members (including Pyle) called National Health in 1977. Not surprisingly, their approach was similar and so were the end results. Among music fans they garnered an enormous reputation for their uncompromising flights and swoops of instrumental rock but they didn't spit at anybody nor wear safety pins or swear on television, so the record companies didn't want to know. Finally, Charly Records took the plunge and released their tremendous first album. Pyle's crisp and imaginative drumming, shines through this album and the following one, but they have made little commercial headway. Their leading light, keyboardist Dave Stewart, now makes successful chart singles – grab it where you can, I suppose.

On record

Hatfield and The North (1974), *The Rotters Club* (1975), *National Health* (1977 – in particular *Tenemos Roads*), *Of Queues And Cures* (1978).

Frank Ricotti

Top flight British acoustic and tuned percussionist whose great versatility can be heard on:
Kids Stuff Babe Ruth (1976), *Waves* Mike Batt (1980), *Graham Bonnet* (1977), *For Girls Who Grow Plump In The Night* Caravan (1973), *Phantasmagoria* Curved Air (1972), *Rendezvous* Sandy Denny (1977), *Weren't Born A Man* Dana Gillespie (1973), *The News* Lindisfarne (1979), *Guitar Syndicate* Hank Marvin (1977), *Water Bearer* Sally Oldfield (1978), *Night Owl* (1979) & *Snakes and Ladders* (1980) by Gerry Rafferty, *Jack The Toad* Savoy Brown (1973), *Rockin' All Over The World* (1977) & *If You Can't Stand The Heat* (1978) by Status Quo, *Six Wives Of Henry VIII* (1973) & *Criminal Record* (1977) by Rick Wakeman.

Bruce Rowland

Took over early on from Kenny Slade in the Greaseband with Alan Spenner (guitar), Henry McCulloch (guitar), Tommy Eyre (keyboards) and Chris Stainton (bass). Stainton switched to keyboards and Spenner to bass, when Eyre left. Joe Cocker took them on as his support band, but they were more than backing musicians, they were the bedrock on which his career was founded and whether he would have succeeded without them is debatable. A check on Cocker's career since he ditched them in 1970 may go some way to answering the question.

Before and during his time with Joe Cocker, Rowland and other Greasebanders worked with Wynder K. Frog whose keyboardist Mick Weaver joined Traffic after Winwood left. After leaving the Greaseband, Rowland had stints with Terry Reid, Gallagher and Lyle and the ambitious Slim Chance led by Ronny Lane, before replacing Dave Mattacks in Fairport Convention, with whom he stayed from 1975-1979, when the group finally packed up. Rowland has also done a lot of session work, including the *Jesus Christ Superstar* album.

On record

The Grease Band (1971), *Joe Cocker* (1970), *Jesse Ed Davis* (1971), *Gallagher and Lyle* (1972), *Willie And The Lap Dog* (1973), *Speeds* (1973) & *Last Cowboy* (1974) all by Gallagher & Lyle, *La Booga Rooga* Andy Fairweather Low (1975), *Another Time, Another Place* Roxy Music (1974), *In Search Of Eddie Riff* Andy MacKay (1974), *Mind Your Own Business* Henry McCulloch (1975), *Anymore For Anymore* Slim Chance (1974), *One World* John Martyn (1977), *Rising For The Moon* (1975), *Tour Sampler* (1975), *Gottle O'Geer* (1976), *Bonny Bunch Of Roses* (1977), *Tipplers Tales* (1978) & *Farewell, Farewell* (1979) all by Fairport Convention, *Swarbrick* (1976), *Swarbrick 2* (1977) & *Lift The Lid And Listen* (1978) all by Dave Swarbrick.

Bruce Rowland also played in various line-ups of Heavy Jelly in 1970. Starting out as a record review hoax everyone from Jimi Hendrix to Jimmy Cagney was rumoured to be in the group. However, a band did emerge, which included John Morshead (guitar), Alex Dmochowski (bass), Chris Woods (wind) and Jackie Lomax on vocals among others; a single was released, but an album wasn't, although it had been recorded.

Alan Schwartzberg

A very versatile and adaptable

Jerry Shirley

American session/touring drummer – how else could you describe someone who has appeared on albums by Grace Jones and Mountain? Nearly all these listings represent a separate genre or sub-genre of popular music.

On record

Heavy Metal BeBop (on *East River*) The Brecker Brothers (1978), *Portrait Gallery* Harry Chapin (1975), *Goes To Hell* (1976) and *Lace and Whiskey* (1977) by Alice Cooper, *Fearless* Tim Curry (1979), *Blue Lights In The Basement* Roberta Flack (1977), *Crash Landing* (1975) and *Midnight Lightning* (1976) by Jimi Hendrix (Two of the slightly more palatable posthumous offerings from the Hendrix estate), *Night Rains* Janis Ian (1979), *Heads* Bob James (1977), *Portfolio* Grace Jones (1977), *Nils* Nils Lofgren (1979), *Veedon Fleece* Van Morrison (1974), *Twin Peaks* Mountain (1977), *Double Trouble* Robert Palmer (1978), *Flesh And Blood* Roxy Music (1980), *Gene Simmons* (1978), *Peter Gabriel* (1977).

Schwartzberg played in one lineup of a prototype jazz-rock band called Dreams which at various times included the Brecker Brothers, Billy Cobham and Steve Gadd.

Danny Seraphine

A one band man, Seraphine has been in Chicago since its formation as Chicago Transit Authority back in 1968. Both Seraphine and Bobby Colomby of Blood, Sweat & Tears, made a big impact in the late Sixties as the first jazz-rock fusionists, Seraphine adding large elements of soul to his drumming style as well. Two factors have served to diminish Seraphine's visibility, the arrival of musicians like Steve Gadd and Billy Cobham and the scorn heaped on Chicago over the years by critics for their insistence on churning out bland seamless and money spinning cabaret music. The gnash of teeth and chewing of pencils is almost guaranteed when rock journalists are faced with *dreck* that sells by the bucket load. The tedious habit of sequential numbering as titles continues – we are up to Chicago 15 or thereabouts (who's counting?) and that says a lot about the music – just one damn album after another.

So it is to the first Chicago album, their debut double of 1968 that must turn for a proper estimation of Seraphine's dramatic and incendiary drumming capabilities. He is exemplary throughout, loud and hard, steaming the band through their simple but exciting brass arrangements and the late Terry Kath's ferocious guitar sound. *Liberation* and *I'm A Man* throw all styles into the melting pot – soul, rock, jazz and latin. Everything that they've done since, could have been a different band – and musically they were.

John Shearer

A most adept drummer, very visual, yet at the same time controlled, whose most noticeable work from the public's point of view has been on stage and record with the Steve Hackett Band and also Moon. Shearer has been playing since he was 12, in trios, dance bands, anything and everything, just to get the experience of playing, for which there is no substitute. Very much the showman, Shearer used to be "the funny drummer" in a knockabout cabaret act called Airport, in much the same vein as Russ Abbott, who performed a similar function in The Black Abbotts, before giving up drumming and going on to a successful career as a solo comedian with his own T.V. show.

As well as his stage and extensive session work, Shearer teaches percussion, endorses Ludwig drums through drum clinics and has had his own *ad hoc* jazz-funk band Full Treatment. He sits behind a massive double bass drum Ludwig set up with 24 drums and 24 cymbals. No, he's not the drummer spoken of earlier in the Heavy Metal Section – John Shearer knows what he's about, using all the percussion at his disposal with intelligence and panache. Having said that, he is now actually working with a HM band called Wolf.

On record

Spectral Mornings Steve Hackett (1979), *Turning The Tide* Moon (1977). Session work includes percussion with the Sutherland Brothers and Quiver.

Jerry Shirley

Prior to joining Humble Pie in 1969 with Steve Marriott, Peter Frampton and Greg Ridley on bass, Shirley had played in Apostolic Intervention, The Wages Of Sin and Little Women. Kicking off with pretensions of being Britain's answer to The Band, Humble Pie eventually found success as a hard-driving blues boogie band on such albums as *Performance* (1971), *Rock On* (1971) and *Smokin'* (1972), notching up impressive U.S. sales. They moved intelligently through the spectra of Marriott's gritty R&B influences and Frampton's cleaner rock sounds, going progressively heavier once ex-Colosseum guitarist Dave Clempson replaced Frampton. The albums mentioned above, while definitive statements of the band overall, tended to suffer from a muffled dragging drum sound, as did all their work before *Thunderbox* (1974), by no means their best effort, but the drum sound at least was much brighter and less muddy.

When Humble Pie wisely disbanded in 1975, Shirley formed Natural Gas with ex-Colosseum bassist Mark Clarke. One very average album released in 1976 was enough. Shirley worked with Sammy Hagar on *Nine On A Ten Scale* (1976), but since then it's mainly been rumours of a Humble Pie reunion and not much else.

Mike Shrieve

After the first two albums with Santana, Shrieve (then only seventeen) became a household name in music circles – lynchpin and anchor man of one of rock's finest ever percussion sections with the amazing Mike Carabello and Jose Chepito Areas.

Shrieve was with Santana during their finest moments, such as the explosive performance of *Soul Sacrifice* at Woodstock, which made them international stars just as *Going Home* did for *Ten Years After* at the same event. However, a major reshuffle in 1976 saw Shrieve leave the band he had been with since the beginning. His replacement was the equally excellent Graham Lear – Carlos can sure pick 'em.

Shrieve formed Automatic Man with guitarist Pat Thrall playing loud, high energy funk/rock with much technical virtuosity but little feeling. Shrieve left after the first album was released and took up with the magical Japanese composer/percussionist Stomu Yamashta, purveyor of extremely eclectic, but rather inaccessible music. A synthesis of classical, rock and jazz, it was often played out as the backdrop to some inventive multi-media presentations. Yamashta collected an impressive array of musicians around him for his later albums. Apart from Shrieve – Steve Winwood, Al Dimeola, Phil Manzanera and Klaus Schulze.

There was a buzz going around about a new band that Shrieve had put together called Shakers, but nothing has materialised as yet.

On record

Santana (1968), *Abraxas* (1970) – the beginning and as it turned out, the pinnacle of Santa's achievements. By utilising pulsating Latin rhythms – Carlos Santana succeeded masterfully in making his band stand out from the crowd.

Mike Shrieve was on all Santana albums to *Amigos* (1976). He played on *Automatic Man* (1976) and on the following Stomu Yamashta albums *Go* (1976), *Go Too* (1977), *Go Live From Paris* (1978), the first being about the best. He also did a session for Dave Crosby back in 1971 for the album *If I Could Only Remember My Name*.

Chris Slade

A drummer who has many strings to his bow within the business. As a musician, his career takes in Tom Jones and Uriah Heep with Manfred Mann's Earthband sandwiched in between. He is also involved in a West London recording studio and was responsible for the unusual Staccato drums, similar in design to those pioneered by Roger North some years ago. They have horn shaped drum shells which project the sound outwards, rather than downwards on a cadency theory of air being pushed through a controlled, expanding shape, enhancing resonance and sound distribution.

On record

How Come The Sun Tom Paxton (1971), *Earthband* (1972), *Get Your Rocks Off* (1973), *Solar Fire* (1973), *The Good Earth* (1974), *Nightingales & Bombers* (1975), *Roaring Silence* (1976) & *Watch* (1978) all by Manfred Mann, *Falling In Love* Frankie Miller (1979).

Steve Smith

He joined Journey in 1978, replacing Aynsley Dunbar who moved to Jefferson Starship. Smith is a well-schooled drummer who has been playing since he was 9, learning his craft with dedication and care through his youth ending up in the Berklee School in Boston. His early gigs were in jazz with ex-Buddy Rich trumpet player Lin Biviano and also Buddy de Franco, moving into jazz fusion with Jean Luc Ponty in 1976, necessitating an obvious change of style towards busier, more intense percussion. The JLP stint lasted until 1977 when the violinist decided that a change of style needed a change of musicians and Smith was out. He had been increasingly unhappy about being told what to play and when, and a move to Ronnie Montrose's band helped to solve this whilst, at the same time, introducing him to his first spate of out and out rock drumming. Playing support to Journey, Smith made friends with the band and they asked him to join in 1978.

The transition from jazz to rock demanded a much fatter, richer and louder sound than he was getting from his small Gretsch kit and so during his Ponty days, he switched to the large Sonor kit that he still plays.

On record

The post-Dunbar Journey allows for little instrumental rock, focussing as it does on vocalist Steve Perry and limiting the opportunities for free musical expression. Nevertheless, Smith is an excellent drummer and features on all new Journey albums since *Evolution* (1978) and the film score the band recorded in Japan entitled DREAM AFTER DREAM, which Smith reckons is the best he has played on record.

He can also be heard on; *Imaginary Voyage* Jean Luc Ponty (1976).

Ed Spevock

Previously with Pete Brown on his *Not Forgotten Association* album (1973), Spevock was a member of Babe Ruth formed in 1971 with Bernie Marsden (brought in from Wild Turkey and later in Whitesnake) and fronted by Jenny Haan. Never that popular in England, their second album *Amar Caballero* (1973) went gold in Canada. Founder members Dave Hewitt and Jenny Haan left around 1975 and, with two new members, the band carried on for one more album *Kids Stuff* (1976) before disbanding. Spevock has been doing mainly session work in Britain and on the Continent and gigs including Chicken Shack and the Peddlars.

A popular jazz oriented outfit of the Sixties who had three chart hits, The Peddlars moved into the cabaret circuit during the Seventies and have only just disbanded for the last time in 1982, as Roy Phillips, the band's original leader has decided to emigrate.

Henry Spinetti

Currently Eric Clapton's drummer and younger brother of acting star Victor, Henry Spinetti replaced Andrew Steele in the Herd before teaming up with Andy Bown also of the Herd and ex-members of Amen Corner to form Judas Jump. A so-called supergroup at the time, they were anything but and when they broke up, two singles and an album later, Spinetti went into session work. His touring work after Judas Jump included Hustler and more recently the wonderful Roger Chapman Shortlist band before he replaced Jamie Oldaker in the Clapton entourage. He has had an illustrious session career and was particularly impressive on Clapton's double live offering *Just One Night* (1980) and on the tour of the same year, playing a Premier Resonator kit with extra tom toms.

His recorded output includes: *Whatever's For Us* (1974), *Show Some Emotion* (1977) & *To The Limit* (1978) all by Joan Armatrading, *Chappo* Roger Chapman (1979), *Just One Night* (1980) & *Another Ticket* (1981) by Eric Clapton, *Ride A Rock Horse* Roger Daltrey (1975), *City To City* Gerry Rafferty (1978), *That's What Friends Are For* Georgie Fame (1979), *Silverbird* Leo Sayer (1973), *Rough Mix* Peter Townshend/Ronnie Lane (1977), *Lazy Racer* (1979) & *Formula 2* (1980) by Lazy Racer (with Tim Renwick on guitar and Dave Markee on bass), *Tundra* Chris Stainton's Band (1976).

Ringo Starr

It is probably no coincidence that the two biggest rock bands in history, The Beatles and The Rolling Stones have had direct, unfussy, rocksteady drummers behind them in the shape of Ringo Starr and Charlie Watts.

History has been kind to Ringo Starr the drummer; in the beginning people thought he couldn't play, sentiments which were underlined in the mid-Sixties when rock produced virtuoso drummers like Ginger Baker and Mitch Mitchell. And then in the general reappraisal of the Beatles coming as the frantic Sixties gave way to the laid back Seventies, producers in America started jumping up and down telling drummers to "play like Ringo", and it was boom time for the blanket and paper towel manufacturers. But, of course, the only person who can play like Ringo is Ringo; there was no way that his feeling and enthusiasm for drumming which comes across so strongly on the records, could be duplicated. You can *sound* like Ringo, but you can't *play* like him – and it was the way he played and the spirit of the execution that made him such a great drummer. Therefore the legacy could only be a distorted compromise, stifling, tight chested, choked drumming with no definition. The trend has only recently begun to be reversed by the likes of Phil Collins, Bill Bruford and Simon Phillips who have helped put the brightness back into percussion.

But Ringo remains a first rate rock 'n' roll drummer – virtually everything he did had something to recommend it – *There's A Place, I Want To Hold Your Hand, I Should Have Known Better, Anytime At All,* the tom-tom fills on the *Sgt. Pepper* album and so on, right through the catalogue.

And probably just as important in the history of drums and drumming, as his performances, was his endorsement of Ludwig drums. In 1962 he was persuaded by Gerry Evans, the West End drum retailer, to trade in his Premier for a £275 Ludwig, ludicrously priced at the time because of import controls. His endorsement of Ludwig virtually saved the makers of the worlds finest hardware from going bankrupt. Ringo Starr to this day, is one of the very few drummers whose endorsement has had a significant impact on sales.

Jim Keltner was one of those drummers driven crazy by demands to play like Ringo. The two drummers first played together at the famous Bangla Desh concert in 1972 and have been firm friends for many years, doing sessions as Thunder (Ringo) and Lightning (Jim).

Did Ringo play the drums on all Beatles records? There's one drummer in New York apparently, who claims to have done the lot, but the truth of the matter is that a session drummer called Andy White did the album cut of *Love Me Do* (but not the single which was Ringo), Paul McCartney did *Back In The USSR* and *The Ballad Of John And Yoko,* and Ringo did everything else.

Darrell Sweet

Darrell Sweet of Nazareth – another band the critics love to hate – has been with them since the beginning and now eleven years and fifteen million albums later, he's still there, doing his job with calm professionalism and content to remain fairly anonymous within the security of a band that is still pulling in the crowds. Originaly called The Shadettes, they changed names in 1969 and turned professional in 1971. Since then, they have worked hard and played aggressively all over the world, making up in effort what they have obviously lacked in skill and imagination.

In fact Sweet had a good technical training and his skills are under-used in Nazareth, although he comes through better on the Jeff Baxter-produced *Malice In Wonderland* (1980), percussion-conscious Baxter giving Sweet more room for manoeuvre. *The Fool Circle* (1981) is an attempt to move away from their stodgy riff-laden image. Sweet plays Ludwig drums.

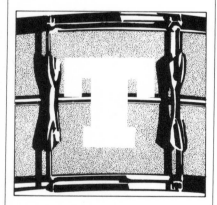

Roger Taylor

Fiery in temperament and aggressive in concert, Queen's Roger Taylor is the driving force behind the world's most extravagant over-the-top rock act – everything to excess – record production sound – stage act – equipment carried (over 70 tons to South America) – records sold and money earned. Yet Taylor keeps a healthy perspective on all this megastardom wrapped up in satin tour jackets, as he said to Melody Maker recently "Here I am, just a bloody rock 'n' roll drummer and all these thousands of kids going crackers. It doesn't seem right somehow, with Britain in a re-

cession".

Taylor went to University to study dentistry, switched to biology and came out with a degree essential if you want to dissect a frog. However, Taylor was more into music than murder – he had a band called Smile in the late Sixties with Brian May. A sub-Cream outfit they released a single called *Earth* in 1969. During the day, May was a shop assistant in a men's clothing store and a frequent customer in outlandish garb was one, F. Mercury, who wanted to be a rock star – and it all came out in the wash as Queen.

Something of a drum connoisseur with a collection of ten Ludwig kits, Taylor branched out into the solo market, with a rather messy over-eclectic album called *Fun In Space* which he wrote, arranged, produced and played all the instruments. However, it seems as long as Queen rules, Taylor will be sitting on the throne thundering away with all the confidence, skill and precision of a musician who has been at the very top for nearly a decade. He is particularly effective on Queen's best album *Sheer Heart Attack* (1974).

Chester Thompson

Since Phil Collins' move up front, Chester Thompson has moved into one of the percussion slots, adding kinetic energy and dynamism to Genesis' stage show. On record, Thompson's electrifying percussive skills shine on Weather Report's *Black Market* (1976), when Thompson was one of the many illustrious drummers to have filled that spot. Acutely aware of the awesome talents around him, Thompson is constantly "listening', pushing and prompting, wearing the mantle of engineer and pilot with confidence. One minute his rhythms are percolating beneath the main themes, next he is riding high over the music urging it along and cutting through with the high ringing tone of his Pearl drums, *Gibraltar* being a good example. Utilising heavier and more funky patterns, Thompson is equally effective on Zappa's live

album *Roxy And Elsewhere* (1974) – also *One Size Fits All* (1974), *Bongo Fury* (1975) and Steve Hackett's *Please Don't Touch* (1978) where he contributes percussion.

Paul Thompson

Since he came down from Newcastle in 1971, Paul Thompson has been associated with Roxy Music and many of its variants and off-shoots; the Bryan Ferry Band, Phil Manzanera's 801 and Andy Mackay solo albums.

Collectively and individually, Roxy Music have been a potent influence on much of the latter day music scene in Britain – the decadence and aloofness of Ferry's lyrical imagery, the techno-tribal African sound experimentations of Brian Eno and the machine gun attack of Paul Thompson, which has been heard the length and breadth of the British new wave/pop sounds for the past three or four years. It was Roxy Music's drive and energy that made their early material so distinctive, particularly *Amazonia, Serenade* and *Street Life* on *Stranded* (1973) where Thompson's drumming served as the spark that set the whole band on fire and secured his reputation as a percussionist of great stature. Apart from his work with Roxy Music, Thompson displays his versatility on Phil Manzanera's *Diamond Head* (1975), with music combining Latin and hard rock influences, an excellent album throughout. Other Thompson work on record includes: *Here Come The Warm Jets* Brian Eno (1974), *Those Foolish Things* (1973), *Another Time, Another Place* (1974), *Let's Stick Together* (1976) & *In Your Mind* (1977) all by Bryan Ferry, *In Search of Eddie Riff* (1974) & *Resolving Contradiction* (1978) by Andy Mackay, *Listen Now* Phil Manzanera (1977).

The Roxy Music live album *Viva* (1976) clearly demonstrates the explosive nature of the band on stage.

Rob Townsend

A Leicester based R&B band called the Farinas evolved into the Roaring Sixties and finally emerged as Family in 1966, whose first of many line-ups was Roger Chapman (vocals), Charlie Whitney (guitar), Tony Ashton (keyboards), Jim Cregan (bass/guitar), Ric Grech (bass), Jim King

(Brass/woodwind) and Rob Townsend who remained ever-present throughout the band's seven year history.

A band full of intelligence, wit, originality and above all, talent and excitement, they had all the ingredients that should have secured their success. However, although they were enormously popular in Britain, they never cracked the American market, mainly because their rather wild, buccaneering personalities resulted in various incidents which precluded a further assault on the U.S. after their first abortive tour. Poor production and mixing, sometimes let them down on record, but they were a force to be reckoned with on stage, the focal point being the ever ebullient and manic Roger Chapman, who wrote most of the band's material with Charlie Whitney.

Behind all the whirlwind of activity, sat Rob Townsend, whose sharp, incisive drumming was a crucial part of the overall sound, either stabbing viciously through great songs like *Burlesque* or rambling menacingly beneath *Weaver's Answer,* both chart singles. Townsend was the anchor man tying down the sound, charting it nimbly through the melodic and lyrical storms created by Chapman and Whitney. This role was more important in Family than in most bands, because each musician was a multi-instrumentalist and through swapping around, they sometimes played without a bass guitar. To help him fill out the sound, Townsend started using a 26in Ludwig bass drum, one of the few drummers using such a large kick drum in the Sixties. Ironically, he had previously used one of the smallest, a mere 18in. Finding a stable bass player was always a problem for Family – Jim Cregan, Ric Grech, John Wetton and John Weider all taking on the job at some time. Constantly striving for perfection and never content to stand still, by 1973 the band realised it wasn't making sufficient progress and called it a day, ironically after a successful British tour.

Townsend moved to Medicine Head, originally an R&B duo who expanded their line-up in the early Seventies and were noted for their economic, sparse sound to which Townsend was able to add his characteristic rhythmic understatements. Later he was re-united with ex-Family members Charlie Whitney and Charlie McCracken in Axispoint and in 1982 replaced Hughie Flint in

the Blues Band.

On record

The definitive Family albums are *Music In A Doll's House* (1968) and *Fearless* (1971). *Best Of Family* (1974) contains many of their classic songs, but Family were really best experienced when they got it together on stage, which admittedly was not on each and every occasion, but when they did, it was phenomenal to watch.

Maureen Tucker

Within rock and its environs, women musicians have lamentably been a rare breed for reasons probably best explained by sociologists. And if you try and identify women *drummers,* you are well and truly in a wasteland. Once you get past the following, it becomes a job for the most experienced rock statisticians; Karen Carpenter, Alice de Buhr (Fanny), Denise Dufort (Girlschool), Sandy West (the Runaways), Honey Lantree of the Honeycombs, (a one-hit wonder Sixties pop band) and a jazz percussionist called Susan Evans who has worked with Billy Cobham, Jack de Johnette, Gil Evans, Diana Ross and Judy Collins.

However, the decision to isolate Maureen Tucker in this listing, is no mere desperate search for a token woman, for Ms Tucker was the primitive, reductionist, tribal beat behind the Velvet Underground, a band of inestimable influence on Seventies music through to the new wave/punk explosion, via David Bowie and Roxy Music.

The music of the Velvet Underground was chaotic, disturbing and fractured, out of step with everything that was going on in the mid-Sixties, reviled and then forgotten, but in the urban angst of the late Seventies, now hauntingly relevant.

All their recorded work was urgent and volatile, whether guided by Lou Reed or in tandem with the equally audacious and imaginative John Cale – *White Light/White Heat, Venus In Furs, Sunday Morning, The Gift, Sister Ray* and *After Hours,* superbly sung by Maureen Tucker herself. She laid down beats of quintessential simplicity and solidity (if not always careful about regular time and pulse).

After the band broke up, Mo Tucker dived into obscurity, but has recently re-emerged with the LA band, Dream Syndicate.

Roger Taylor

On record

The Velvet Underground with Nico (1967), *White Light, White Heat* (1967), *Velvet Underground* (1969) and the excellent double live album *Velvet Underground Live* (1974) are the classic albums. *Velvet Underground* (1976) in the MGM/Polydor special series, has some of the tracks mentioned above taken from the first three albums.

Twink (John Alder)

Doyen of the beer drinking, urban guerilla circuit, Twink started out in an early Sixties outfit called Dane Stephens and the Deep Beats, who signed to Decca in 1964 and changed their name to the Fairies, a first rate R&B band, with Mick Weaver on keyboards. The group split in 1965, Twink joining Keith West and Steve Howe in the In Crowd. A name change to Tomorrow signalled a complete musical *volte face* and they became one of Britain's premier psychedelia bands with classics like *My White Bicycle*. At the same time, vocalist West had an individual hit with *Excerpt From A Teenage Opera* and this tended to push the others into a subordinate role which caused resentments and finally a split. This was unfortunate, as the band had it in them to be big leaguers. Twink then spent about eighteen months in the Pretty Things until November 1969, when he left to record a solo album *Think Pink*.

From here on in, Twink's musical adventures became increasingly less fashionable. He teamed up with Steve Took in Shagrat and then played in the Pink Fairies, which was basically Mick Farren and the Social Deviants without Farren. Like Edgar Broughton and Hawkwind the PFs saw themselves as "a band of the people", often playing free concerts and benefits on the fringes of main "establishment" events. Twink recorded their first album and then took off on a hippy sojourn to Morocco, but not before playing the only two gigs of Stars, Syd Barrett's one foray into the public eye since Pink Floyd. Twink returned for a PF reunion in 1975 and then became caught up in punk. The Chiswick label recorded two Twink bands between 1977-1978 – The Rings and Twink and the Fairies, before Twink skipped off to Belgium and hasn't been heard of since.

On record

A quasi-legendary figure on the London rock scene for well over a decade, he can be heard on: *Emotions* (1967) & *SF Sorrow* (1968) by The Pretty Things, *Tomorrow* (1968), *Never Never Land* The Pink Fairies (1977), *Captain Lockheed And The Starfighters* Robert Culvert (1974).

Santa Barbara Machinehead – a quintessentially obscure British blues band who recorded three tracks which appeared on a blues anthology album in 1968 – *but* Twink was on drums with Jon Lord, Ron Wood and Kim Gardner on bass who was in the Birds, Creation and Ashton, Gardner and Dyke.

Mick Underwood

Gillan's Underwood has an impressive list of credentials linking him to rock heavyweights back to the Sixties; the Outlaws with Ritchie Blackmore (1964-65); the Herd with Peter Frampton (1966), Episode Six wtih Ian Gillan and Roger Glover (1968) and Quatermass (1969-71) with ex-Big Three bassist John Gustafson.

Underwood was with the Herd only in their early days before they were a pop success and the two year gap before he joined Episode Six, represented a period when he dropped out of the business altogether. His career continued into the Seventies, but he was unfortunate in that none of the ensembles he was associated with were ultimately successful; Paul Rodgers' Peace (1971), Sammy (1972) and Strapps who struggled on for five years without ever breaking through, although they accrued some success in Japan. Underwood replaced Mark Nauseef in Gillan during 1979 and has played on all their albums since *Mr. Universe*.

On record

Quatermass (1970), *Sammy* (1972), *Strapps* (1976) & *Secret Damage* (1977) by Strapps, *Mr. Universe* (1979), *Glory Road* (1980) & *Future Shock* (1981) all by Gillan.

Christian Vander

Leader and all-pervading influence in Magma, doyen of the French underground for many years, with a brand of classically-oriented pomp rock whose inner complexities almost defy description.

Vander himself came from an impressive jazz background; taught by Chet Baker and Elvin Jones and sideman to John Coltrane and Chick Corea. Utilising *avant-garde* jazz and classical influences (e.g. Ornette Coleman and Stockhausen), Vander masterminded the creation of Magma dedicated to the weaving of apocalyptic science fiction tapestries such as *1001 Degrees Centigrade* concerning a battle between Earth and a rival planet sung in a language invented by Vander. And so on – rigidly controlled, deadly serious, but finally uninspiring and pretentious, although Vander is an excellent percussionist with much musical intelligence.

On record

Magma is Magma is Magma, all their albums are similar in tone and effect, *1001 Degrees Centigrade* (1971 – and only released in France) and *Live* (1975), are two of their more accessible offerings.

Pierre Van der Linden

Another fine European percussionist,

Mick Underwood

Pierre Van der Linden

he played in some of Holland's most noted rock bands, such as the Hunters and Brainbox with Jan Akkerman. After a period in the Dutch version of Hair, playing in the stage group, Akkerman renewed his partnership with the drummer, inviting him to join Focus in 1971, one of the best bands ever to come out of Holland.

A very popular band who toured extensively in the early Seventies with a brand of classically-oriented jazz/rock much beloved by Continental outfits. Over the years, the individual talents of all the musicians were often showcased within the context of the long improvisational pieces that were the hallmark of the band. As a soloist, Van der Linden was very Baker-influenced which meant lots of rolling tom-tom work and fast bass drum patterns essential in the maintenance of a powerful rock foundation from which flowed the frenetic musicianship of Jan Akkerman and multi-instrumentalist Thijs Van Leer.

By 1973, Van der Linden was replaced by Colin Allen; he came in again briefly before being permanently superceded by David Kemper. His work since then has included the *Shot Into The Blue* album for the Dutch band Sveet D. Busker.

On record

He was with Focus from *Moving Waves* (1971) to *Ship Of Memories* (1974) and it is *Moving Waves* which best demonstrates what an asset he was to the band. Jan Akkerman has

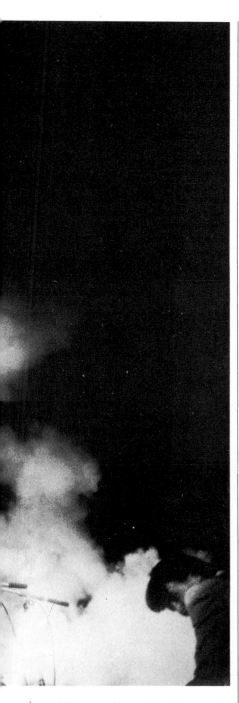

musicians in Joe Walsh's Barnstorm in 1972.

He featured on *Barnstorm* (1972), Walsh's superb soft rock album, probably his best, and on most of Walsh's subsequent solo albums, although Vitale actually left the second version of Barnstorm to go solo himself. Two solo albums have emerged, *Rollercoaster Weekend* (1975) with his former boss and Rick Derringer on guitar and *Plantation Harbour* (1982). Produced and engineered by Bill Szymczyk, *Barnstorm* was mainly recorded at the Caribou Ranch Studio in Colorado, which was only half finished at the time. Upstairs, the finest equipment that money could buy and downstairs, sawdust.

On record

Vitale's hard, steady drumming can be heard on the following: *One Of These Nights* Eagles (1975), *All Alone In The End Zone* Jay Ferguson (1976), *Netherlands* Dan Fogelberg (1977), *Illegal Stills* Steve Stills (1976), *Long May You Run* Stills/Young Band (1976), *Barnstorm* (1972), *The Smoker You Drink* (1973), *So What* (1975), *You Can't Argue With A Sick Mind* (1975) & *But Seriously Folks* (1978) all by Joe Walsh.

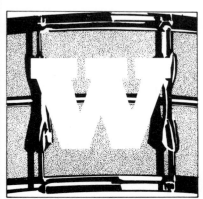

Narada Michael Walden

Born in Michigan in 1952, the phenomenal Michael Walden played in a variety of bands before joining the Mahavishnu Orchestra in 1973, including a drum/organ duo called the Ambassadors, a quasi-Electric Flag band called Promise and the New McGuire Sisters led by former Johnny Winter guitarist Sandy Torano.

After John McLaughlin broke up the original Mahavishnu Ork, he formed a greatly expanded Mark II with a string section. He brought the

ensemble to London to record *Apocalypse* (1974) with the London Symphony Orchestra. Walden also recorded *Visions Of The Emerald Beyond* (1975), which if it had nothing else, demonstrated Walden's thunderous fusion drumming style, using twin kick drums. While in London, Walden was asked by Jeff Beck to do sessions for *Wired* (1976). Walden then had a stint in the Tommy Bolin band until the young guitarist's tragic death.

At this point, Walden, also a composer, keyboard player and vocalist, decided to strike out on his own and has released a series of fusion/funk albums, which although patchy, contain some stunning material. The following represent the best tracks on the albums, both from a compositional and percussion point of view. Guests on his albums have included a triumvirate of outstanding guitarists, Jeff Beck, Carlos Santana and Ray Gomez and they also appear variously on these tracks: *White Night* (1977), *Garden Of Love Light* (1977) & *Saint And The Rascal* (1977) all by Garden Of Love Light, *I Remember* (1978) & *Oneness – Cry* (1978) both by I Cry, I Smile, *They Want The Feeling* (1979), *I Don't Want Nobody Else* (1979) & *The Dance Of Life* (1979) by Awakening, *Victory Suite* Victory (1980).

On record

Apart from the listing above, Michael Walden can be heard on: *The Teaser* Tommy Bolin (1975), *Loading Zone* Roy Buchanan (1977), *My Spanish Heart* Chick Corea (1977), *Exposure* Bob Fripp (1979), *Jaco Pastorius* (1976), *Black Market* Weather Report (1976).

By Gadd, this guy is good.

Ian Wallace

The Warriors were a beat group from Accrington, in the North of England, who made one single for Decca in 1964 called *You Came Along*. Jon Anderson, later of Yes, was the vocalist and the drummer was Ian Wallace, who was so young when the Warriors cut that record, that he had to ask his mum if he could go along to the session. Fortunately his mum said "yes" and since then, it has been up all the way for this extremely capable, highly regarded, powerhouse drummer who continues to be much in demand.

After the Warriors, Wallace went into sessions and worked with Neil Innes before replacing Andrew McCulloch in King Crimson in 1970.

used him on three solo albums; the excellent *Profilè* (1972), *Eli* (1977) and *Jan Akkerman* (1978). He also features on Trace's first album (1974) with Rick Van der Linden on keyboards.

Joe Vitale

Part of the Cleveland, Ohio crowd that included Joe Walsh and bassist Kenny Passarelli, Joe Vitale is a multi-instrumentalist who joined these

The band with Boz Burrell (bass/vocals), Mel Collins (saxes/keyboards) and Robert Fripp, toured extensively in the UK and America, recording *Islands* (1971) with its spare, unsatisfactory arrangments and the equally disappointing *Earthband* (1972), a live album.

The underlying problem with the band, was that the chemistry was all wrong; Collins, Burrell and Wallace were just not on the same wavelength as the serious-minded Fripp. Eventually, after a period of increasing acrimony, the band split. Collins, Burrell and Wallace stayed in America, named themselves Snape and teamed up with Alexis Korner and Peter Thorup. Snape was an on-the-road dare game, played between many British bands originating in the Sixties, involving the execution of ever more outrageous dares – flower eating and so on. This gives some indication of where Fripp and the other musketeers fell out.

Wallace came back to England to play with the Chapman-Whitney Streetwalkers, Steve Marriott's All Stars and the Alvin Lee Band, before a move into the big league with Bob Dylan's band in 1978. Since then, Wallace has recorded with David Lindley on his recent and much acclaimed *El Rayo X* album (1981). Such is the power of Wallace's drumming, that on a real pile-driving rocker called *Mercury Blues,* a recording console blew up.

On record

Ian Wallace's recorded output apart from that already mentioned, includes: *Graham Bell* (1972), *Accidentally Born In New Orleans* Alexis Korner (1973), *Brighter Day* Keith Christmas (1974), *Lucky Planet* Neil Innes (1970), *Bump and Grind* Jackson Heights (1973), *Road to Freedom* (1973), *In Flight* (1974) & *Pump Iron* (1975) by the Alvin Lee Band, *Marriott* Steve Marriott (1976), *Streetwalkers* (1974), *Street Legal* Bob Dylan (1978).

Ian Wallace has also played with an *ad hoc* group of musicians who do occasional live gigs called Hinkley's Heroes, which variously includes Boz Burrell, Henry McCulloch, Poli Palmer, Charlie Whitney, Mel Collins, Mitch Mitchell, Roger Chapman and keyboardist Tim Hinkley.

Micky Waller

Possibly one of Britain's most underrated rock drummers over the years.

He made a name for himself in the Sixties with major R&B artists like Cyril Davies, Brian Auger and Long John Baldry in the All Stars, the Trinity and Steampacket, before joining the Jeff Beck Band and recording the astonishing *Truth* album (1968). Beck has played with many of the fierce, hard-nut drummers; Viv Prince and Aynsley Dunbar before Waller; Tony Newman, Cozy Powell and Carmine Appice since – all big personalities in their own way, loud and confident. Only the drummers in Jeff Beck bands tend to remain with their heads above the water musically speaking – everyone else gets submerged. This was very much the case with the *Truth* album, Waller holding his own while the others struggled. It was this battle, however, that made the album so good.

Waller was with Beck for about a year and a half, moving on to Steamhammer, an archetypal late Sixties British blues band. Aware of his abilities through their time together in Steampacket and the Beck Band, Rod Stewart used Micky Waller on his first four solo albums, but it was the first three, and in particular *Every Picture Tells A Story* (1971), which represent Micky Waller's finest moments.

Rarely can a drummer have brought such power and irresistible energy to an album as Waller did to *EPTAS.* It launched Stewart as a major solo artist and secured the album a place in every serious rock fan's collection. One has only to think of the force of the title track and *Losing You,* where the drums are at their most audible and memorable, to realise what a contribution he made. A rock album made of granite and easily Rod Stewart's best.

The general obscurity that Waller fell into after his sessions with Stewart can only be regarded as astonishing. He can still be seen around London pubs playing blues gigs, such as in Alexis Korner's all-star Rocket 88.

On record

An Old Raincoat Won't Ever Let You Down (1970), *Gasoline Alley* (1970), *Every Picture Tells A Story* (1971), *Never A Dull Moment* (1972) (particularly the clean, incisive snaps of *You Wear It Well*).

Andy Ward

Ward, Doug Ferguson (bass) and Andy Latimer (guitar) of Camel, came together in Brew during 1968, and

backed Philip Goodhand Tait before joining with keyboardist Peter Bardens in Camel, now embarking on their tenth anniversary tour. Camel have always had a hard core of loyal supporters without ever exactly setting the world on fire, playing jazz-oriented orchestrated rock pieces, the most famous being *Snow Goose* (1975) which brought the band's first chart successes in the UK and America. A Pearl drummer, Ward has provided lots of precise, controlled jazz feels, helping to save Camel from veering too often into the realms of pomp rock stodge.

On record

I'll Write A Song Philip Goodhand Tait (1971), *Snow Goose* (1975), *Moonmadness* (1976) and *A Live Record* (1978) by Camel, all have points to commend them from a percussion point of view.

Bill Ward

A real Titan on drums and to some extent underrated, Bill Ward was for ten years half of the frenzied rhythm section that made up Black Sabbath, the band who laid all the ground rules for heavy metal. Initially, Sabbath came together in Birmingham as Earth from the amalgam of two bands, Mythology (Ward and Tony Iommi) and Rare Breed (Geezer Butler and Ozzy Osbourne).

Collectively and individually, their reputation on the Birmingham Club scene was enormous. Bill Ward used to have drum battles with the excellent Pete York during the jam sessions that York organised in Birmingham and London, where Ian Paice and Keef Hartley would do the honours.

As Earth, they played the Hamburg dates breaking the house record at the notorious Star Club. They did so many sets there, that one whole set might just be a guitar solo, another would be a Bill Ward solo. Despite vitriolic attacks by the critics and messy management problems, Black Sabbath turned out one hit album after another, producing in the process such HM classics as *Paranoid, War Pigs* and *Sweet Leaf.* Every concert is the same: 1. It's a sell-out, 2. Everyone goes ape from first note to last, 3. It's loud. And behind it all, sits Bill Ward, committing mayhem on his Slingerland kit – that was until the end of 1980, when after a decade of thunderous percussion, he dramatically and without fanfare, left the band for personal and family reasons. Carmine Appice's younger brother Vinnie, took over.

On record

Paranoid (1970), *Master of Reality* (1971), and *Sabbath, Bloody Sabbath* (1973), say it all – even in the titles, apart from this review of *Sabotage* (1975). "If Hitler had needed music to invade Poland and if Sabbath had been around, this is the album he would have used". Possibly the heaviest rock album of all time.

Charlie Watts

It took a lot of persuading to get Charlie Watts to give up his £14 a week job as a trainee design artist and throw in his lot with a bunch of half-starved yobs, none of whom his jazz friends thought had a prayer in the music business. He had already turned down Alexis Korner's offer of a job in Blues Incorporated, although he did do a few gigs until Ginger Baker came in. Eventually, it was a combination of Brian Jones, Alexis Korner

and his wife Bobbie, that made him change his mind. Early in 1963, he became a Rolling Stone. What emerged, was one of the classic rhythm sections in rock – Charlie Watts and Bill Wyman as serious and unwavering in the thrust and precision of their music – nearly twenty years on – as their icy on-stage demeanour.

Charlie Watts retains all his jazz allegiances – his hero is Charlie Parker, but only spiritually and emotionally, for Watts' style is as breathtakingly simple as Parker's was complex. Honed-to-the-bone clipped jazz-feel chops on his trusty Gretsch kit with fill-ins rare as precious metal he leaves in his wake a trail of rock landmarks which add up to some of the most compelling white R&B drumming of all time – *Satisfaction, Get Off My Cloud, Route 66, Have You Seen Your Mother Baby (Standing In The Shadows), Under My Thumb, Street Fighting Man, Brown Sugar, Moonlight Mile, Tumbling Dice, Start Me Up*. For sure, that intro to *Honky Tonk Women* will *Not Fade Away* – ever.

John Weathers

John "Pugwash" Weathers is part of the Welsh connection comprising Phil Ryan and Taff Williams, formerly of Man, and Gary Pickford Hopkins, who have all played in bands together in the Sixties and early Seventies.

It all started when the lads from Neath calling themselves Eyes of Blue, won the Melody Maker group contest for 1966. They signed to Mercury under the guidance of Rod Stewart's producer Lou Reizner and recorded *Crossroads Of Time* (1968), the title track written by Graham Bond who also penned the sleeve notes. *In Fields of Ardath* (1969) was their next effort, at which point Weathers split for Pete Brown's Piblokto. 1970 was reunion time for Weathers, Ryan and Hopkins in Ancient Grease until, always very aware of his drumming talent, Graham Bond recruited Pugwash Weath-

Bill Ward

ers for his short-lived Holy Magick Band, threatening the drummer on occasion to "turn you into a frog" if he misbehaved himself. The boys from the valley got together again in Big Sleep during 1971 until Weathers took on his most prolonged commitment, with Gentle Giant formed by the Shulman Brothers from the ashes of an undistinguished pop outfit called Simon Dupree and the Big Sound, notable only for their 1968 hit single *Kites*. Weathers stayed with Gentle Giant from 1973-1980, during which time he had yet another recording interlude with his old mates in the Neutrons. Always an acquired taste, Gentle Giant garnered modest cult success around the world, playing quite innovative well crafted and well executed "progressive" rock, reminiscent of Yes and King Crimson, shot through with the classical influences often associated with this genre. The quality of the musicianship was never less than superb, Weathers particularly skilful on *Octopus* (1973), his first album with the band, full on unusual time signatures and intricate structures.

On record

Crossroads Of Time (1968) & *In Fields Of Ardath* (1969) by Eyes Of Blue, *Women And Children First* Ancient Grease (1970), *Bluebell Wood* Big Sleep (1971), *We Put Our Magick On You* Graham Bond (1971), *My Last Band* Pete Brown (1977 – includes early Piblokto tracks).

Weathers plays on all Gentle Giant albums from *Octopus* onwards. *Free Hand* (1975) is another recommended album, more accessible than *Octopus* but still retaining the complex time structures on arrangements at which Weathers is so adept.

Max Weinberg

"Mighty" Max Weinberg went from New Jersey to New York to study with ace soul drummer Bernard Purdie. He answered an ad, in Village voice seeking a drummer and a keyboard player. He got one job, Roy Bittan got the other. The advertiser? Bruce Springsteen.

Weinberg, with a wealth of professional experience behind him, including the orchestra pit of GODSPELL, is an out and out rocker but much influenced by Sixties Motown drumming. In replacing "Boom Boom" Carter in the E Street Band, Weinberg brought with him a resiliant orchestral approach but more importantly,

an extra drama and tension to music very much dependent on the theatricality, commitment and celebratory nature of its delivery.

All the more remarkable then, that Weinberg's huge sound rapping out those wonderful crescendos and climaxes should all be executed on a tiny four-piece Ludwig – he sits perched on the drum riser surrounded by space. "I've got four drums, anything else is redundant, besides I tend to trip over things."

On record

Born To Run (1975), *Darkness On The Edge Of Town* (1978), *The River* (1980 – note the Motown-influenced intro on *Hungry Heart*. Weinberg's ambient drum sound makes marvellous listening). Also appears on: *You're Never Alone With A Schizo* Ian Hunter (1979), *Hearts Of Stone* Southside Johnny (1978).

Alan White

In 1968, Colin Gibson from the much respected Skip Bifferty, teamed up with Alan White to form Happy Magazine, which became Gryphon with the addition of vocalist Graham Bell. Unfortunately, Gryphon had a hard time of it; legal hassles with ex-Skip Bifferty manager Don Arden, prevented them from working in Britain, so they had to work abroad, partly subsidised by White's earnings from his Plastic Ono Band session work. He also played on the famous *Live Peace In Toronto* album (1969) with Lennon, Clapton and bassist Klaus Voormann. Gryphon gave up the ghost in 1969, White moving on briefly to Ginger Baker's Airforce and then Balls with Jackie Lomax, Denny Laine, Trevor Burton and Steve Gibbons, which struggled on with this line-up for just over a year, getting nowhere fast, despite its inherent talent. White then embarked on the major part of his career by joining Yes in 1972, when Bill Bruford left – a surprising choice in many respects, considering the sharp contrast in styles, White being basically a rock 'n' roll drummer. He stayed with the band right through to the bitter end, outstaying Jon Anderson, Rick Wakeman, until Geoff Downes and Steve Howe went woodshedding with Asia and Yes became No. Alan White plays Ludwig drums.

On record

Alan White has done sessions for many musicians, including Billy Fury, Georgie Fame, Joe Cocker, Alan Price, Donovan and George Harrison,

plus: *Plastic Ono Band* (1970), *Imgine* John Lennon (1971), *Beginnings* (1977) & *Steve Howe* (1979), *Back Street Crawler* (1973), *Music Machine Patent Pending* Johnny Almond (1969), *Ramshackled* (1976 – this was his own solo album during the time when there was an epidemic of solo albums from individual members of Yes. However, the album was very much better than that introduction would suggest).

Maurice White

One half of Maurice White's career is well known as the man who brought you the percussion-based Earth, Wind and Fire, whose rock/funk sound is as the name suggests – it's solid, it blows up a storm and it cooks. However, prior to the formation of EW&F, White, who studied for three years at the Chicago Music Conservatory, was an ace staff drummer with Chess and Tamla Motown, recording with Curtis Mayfield and the Impressions, the Four Tops, the Supremes, Chuck Berry, Howlin' Wolf, Muddy Waters and Martha and the Vandellas – White played drums on *Dancin' In The Street*. He also backed jazz artists like Sonny Stitt and played with John Coltrane when Elvin Jones went off sick for a while. That experience helped change his whole attitude to life and music, which later manifested itself in the universal brotherhood and spirituality at the root of the EW&F philosophy.

But his big break as a drummer in the public eye, came when he joined the Ramsey Lewis Trio and played on the 1965 smash hit single *The In Crowd*, which won a Grammy award. Originally formed as the Salty Peppers, early EW&F played a lot of loose, free ranging jazz arrangements and it wasn't until White disbanded the original line-up and switched labels, that the music tightened up. The hits started coming and the elaborate stage act developed, including the revolving drum riser.

Although he played drums on *Singasong*, White is now mainly the lead vocalist and percussionist backed by percussion/drummer Ralph Johnson, percussionist Philip Bailey and brother Freddy on drums, who joined in 1974 after spells with Little Feat and Donnie Hathaway among others.

On record

The Best Of Earth, Wind and Fire (1978), *Gratitude* (1975), a double album, one of which is live and is most

Alan White

representative of the overall power of the ensemble.

Terry Williams

Uncompromising hard rock drummer who played in a band called Dream in the late Sixties, with Deke Leonard and Martin Ace, all three coming together later in Man, one of Wales' finest and most famous rock bands.

Man had a tortuous career with rising and falling fortunes and labyrinthine personnel changes – twelve albums and thirteen line-ups. But the whole operation ran like a big family whose sons ran away only to return at some later date as prodigals, welcomed back and reintegrated into the fold once more.

They found foreign parts more welcoming to their brand of passionate, driving rock, particularly Germany, but probably their most successful time was during 1974-75, when they cracked the American market for a short halcyon period. Their current album *Slow Motion* (1974) was played everywhere and they wowed them at Bill Graham's Winterland venue in San Francisco. Boogie from the valley was all the rage. During his time with Man, Wiliams had done some recording work with another Welsh musician, Dave Edmunds, and he joined Rockpile on a permanent basis around 1977.

Subtle As A Flying Mallet (1975) suggests what Rockpile were all about, ferocious, pile-driving rock and roll – Nick Lowe and Terry Williams formed an ultra tight rhythm unit without so much as a hairline crack.

On record

Terry Williams plays on all Man albums, underpinning the music with characteristicaly hypnotic rhythmic structures from *Man* (1970) onwards and all Rockpile albums. Man's *All's Well That Ends Well* (1977 – a live album) was the band's swansong. *Hard Way To Live* is particularly fiery, showing just why Dave Edmunds wanted Terry Williams in his band.

Tony Williams

A genuinely innovative drummer, Tony Williams' influence on fusion music in the Seventies has been enormous in a direct line through Billy Cobham, who regards Williams as his mentor and main inspiration. Cobham extended and developed two vital elements in Williams' pioneering style for the purposes of high energy, incendiary fusion drumming. The first was the very difficult left-right-left-right single stroke roll, a rudiment whose clarity was accentuated by Cobham's style of tuning and which formed the building block of much of his solos and fill-ins. The second was the more complete integration of the bass drum in the execution of cross rhythmic patterns, releasing it more from a mere time-keeping role.

Williams was playing with Miles Davis in 1963 when he was only seventeen (both Williams and Cobham played on the jazz-rock album *Bitches Brew*). He moved in rock circles with Lifetime, featuring John McLaughlin, legendary keyboardist Larry Young and Jack Bruce, who has commented that it was the best band he has ever played in – as anyone who saw them live will testify.

Immediate precursor of the Mahavishnu Orchestra and easily its equal, Lifetime suffered through a combination of ego clashes and a management who had them playing school halls in Hicksville. Williams carried on with two further versions of Lifetime, one with ex-Soft Machine guitarist, Allan Holdsworth.

Ironically, his solo career since, has suffered in much the same way as Billy Cobham's, as he tried to widen the appeal of his music. Fine fusion/funk offerings like *Believe It, Million Dollar Legs,* and *Joy Of Flying*, were

poorly promoted and after the last album, CBS dropped Williams, even though the record sold in excess of 100,000 copies.

What can a poor boy do, except be one of the world's greatest jazz drummers?

On record

Bitches Brew Miles Davis (1970 – must be included here).

Lifetime was not served particularly well on record; the 1975 Polydor release sounded as if the band were standing in the next street, but *Life-* *time* (1975), does give a glimmer of how good this band was. Other Lifetime albums: *Emergency* (1969), *Turn It Over* (1970), *Ego* (1970) & *The Old Bum's Rush* (1972). *Believe It* (1976), *Million Dollar Legs* (1976) & *Joy Of Flying* (1976) all by Tony Williams (an all-star cast including Jan Hammer, Herbie Hancock, Stanley Clarke, George Benson and Ronnie Montrose).

Barrie J. Wilson

In 1962, when B. J. Wilson was fifteen, he joined a top class R&B band from Southend, called the Paramounts with Robin Trower and Gary Brooker. They worked extensively as a unit in their own right but eventually had to back artists like Sandie Shaw in order to survive. B. J. Wilson left the band and became a sideman to Cat Stevens, Lulu and Millie with her backing band, George Bean and the

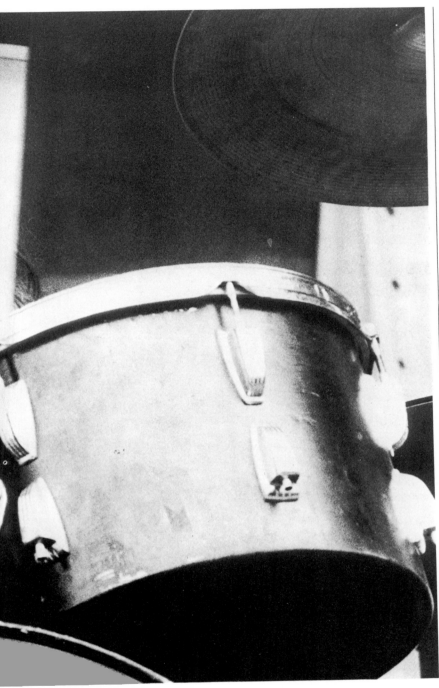

he laid down the drums for the title track. Whatever one may think aesthetically, the dull, thick drum sound was a feature of many albums recorded in the Seventies with the praise or blame for this laid at the feet of Ringo Starr. Engineers and producers muffled drums in a swathe of blankets and tape, to get 'that Ringo Sound'. However, while not denying the totality of Ringo's influence, I would contend that the hit song *With A Little Help From My Friends* was the single most influential record in determining this Seventies drum fashion.

On record

Apart from his work with Procol Harum, B. J. Wilson has appeared on: *Slug Line* John Hiatt (1979), *Double Trouble* Frankie Miller (1978), *Berlin* Lou Reed (1973), *No Ruinous Feud* Incredible String Band (1973), *Leon Russell* (1970).

David "Pick" Withers

Creator of those remarkably seamless, silky, slowburn tempos which are the hallmark of Dire Straits. It is interesting to note how the drums have been brought forward in the mix with each successive record without ever overbalancing the internal dynamics of each song. One of the most distinctive rhythm styles around at the moment, Withers' drumming is equally stunning on Dylan's *Slow Train Coming* (1979) and Bert Jansch's *A Rare Conundrum* (1977).

Robert Wyatt

Labelled as a band who were ahead of its time, Soft Machine was an ideas band whose time never actually arrived. Lurking somewhat bemused on the fringes of the rock scene, they had little allegiance to the British youth culture despite being the darlings of the hippy underground demimonde. Their main inspiration came from avant-garde free jazz and the art/theatre tradition of Surrealism and Dadaism; going some way to explain their popularity in France which stemmed originally from their involvement in a St. Tropez mixed media event that the local police broke up.

Brought together from the petals of Wilde Flowers in 1966, Robert Wyatt, Daevid Allen, Mike Ratledge and

Runners. Then came a phone call from Gary Brooker to audition for Procol Harum as their first drummer, Bobby Harrison had quit in 1967 to form Freedom. B.J. got the job and stayed with them until the end, around 1978. He has always had a very nimble, precise and individualistic sense of dynamics born of schoolday experience in competition pipe drumming and symphonic orchestral percussion. No wonder he felt confident to turn professional at fifteen. His work with Procol Harum

Terry Williams

was exemplary, particularly on *Procol Harum* (1967), *A Salty Dog* (1969) and *Exotic Fruit And Birds* (1974), not forgetting his breath taking outing on the title track of *Broken Barricades* (1974). Only in his later days with Procol Harum, did he introduce soloing into his routine.

During 1969, he played on the super session put together to record Joe Cocker's album *With A Little Help From My Friends*. More particularly,

Kevin Ayers were a unique collection of fierce talents making Soft Machine one of the most important of the Canterbury bands. The band broke up after a bad dose of rock burnout on tour with Jimi Hendrix in America in 1968. Before this, they had already lost Daevid Allen and when Wyatt reformed the band in 1969, Hugh Hopper replaced Kevin Ayers, who could not be persuaded to return, on bass. Wyatt himself left the band for a variety of political and musical reasons in 1971. He went on to form Matching Mole (*machine meule* being French for Soft Machine) and toured briefly with Kevin Ayers and the Whole World.

Wyatt was very much the focal point of Soft Machine; in those early days, ebullient and temperamental. He was known to leave the stage in tears if the sound wasn't right or empty bottles of coke flew over his head in mid-solo. Even during Wilde Flowers days, he would rather sing than play drums, but nevertheless, he was an exceptionally talented and grossly underrated jazz/rock drummer with a big, loose drum sound.

His skills as a drummer have tragically to be written in the past tense, because in 1973, a fall from a window left him paralysed from the waist down, ending this era of his career.

But being a down to earth man with a determination to fight back, he turned his attentions to writing and produced albums like *Rock Bottom* (1974) and *Ruth Is Stranger Than Richard* (1975), with songs of great personal anger and regret and songs of purpose and commitment knocking the chic radicalism of Clash and co. into a cocked hat.

On record

Soft Machine (1968), *Volume 2* (1969) and to a lesser extent *Third* (1970), are all premier examples of English experimental rock with Wyatt outstanding, particularly on the debut album which demonstrated the Softs then were not quite as inaccessible as their critics made out. However, all was not well on *Third*. The best track is Wyatt's *Moon In June*, but Hopper and Ratledge hated it and wouldn't play, so Wyatt had to do it all himself. This prompted the release of a solo album *The End Of An Ear* (1970). The ever-intrepid Giorgio Gomelsky got hold of 1967 demo tapes and released them in France on the Byg label for their 'Rock Generation' series. Again, Wyatt is superb.

Matching Mole released two albums, *Matching Mole* (1972) and *Little Red Record* (1973). Plans were being laid for a third album when the accident happened.

Pete York

Middlesborough born Pete York has been playing drums since he was ten. He was part of the enormously successful Spencer Davis Group laying down those compulsive rock solid beats for classic songs that sound just as good today as when they were first released; *Keep On Running* (1965), *Somebody Help Me* (1966), *Gimme Some Lovin'* (1966) and *I'm A Man* (1967).

When the band broke up in 1969, Pete formed a duo with keyboardist Eddie Hardin, allowing him to expand and develop his already considerable skills. He went to Europe with the Pete York Percussion Band, played with Chris Barber from 1976-79 and now heads his own band once again, New York. He also organised *ad hoc* touring bands with as many as three drummers in the line-ups playing arrangements partly composed by Pete York himself. Keith Moon, Ian Paice, Bill Ward and Keef Hartley were among the drummers concerned.

As a freelance musician, York has recorded and toured with an impressive list of musicians covering a wide cross-section of the popular music scene; Jon Lord, Chris Farlowe, Eric Burdon, Brian Auger, Jack Bruce, Eric Clapton, Memphis Slim, Sonny Boy Williamson, Buddy Guy, Johnny Griffin, Alexis Korner, Philip Catherine and Inex and Charlie Foxx.

Pete York has been heavily involved in the business and teaching side of percussion as well – recording a video drum course and touring the world performing drum clinics for the Pearl Drum Company. Anxious to encourage new drummers, he is also vice-president of the Contemporary Drummers Society and the Pearl Association of Drummers.

Not much in the British public eye of late, due to his overseas work, York remains a committed and popular musician, particularly in Germany, where he conducts his clinics in fluent German. A recent magazine poll there, voted him the third best drummer in the world. On top of all that, he manages to find time to be a restauranteur in Lambourn, Berkshire.

On record

Apart from the Spencer Davis material, Pete York can be heard to particularly good effect on Jon Lord's orchestral/rock piece *Sarabande* (1976).

Randy Zehringer

Randy Zehringer and his brother Rick (who later changed his name to Derringer), started a quasi-bubblegum Ohio band called the McCoys who found themselves, still teenagers, with a hit record on their hands called *Hang On Sloopy* in 1965. They had a few more chart singles then signed to Mercury to try and affect an image change towards what was more fashionable in the late Sixties. The two Mercury albums *Infinite McCoys* (1968) and *Human Ball* (1968), were hard-edged psychedelia which both bombed and finally the band gravitated to backing Johnny Winter, both on stage and record. And a spirited, fireball outfit it was too, as they showed on *Johnny Winter And* (1971) especially *Guess I'll Go Away* and *Rock And Roll Hoochie Koo*.

INDEX OF DRUMMERS

A

Aldridge, Tommy
Allen, Colin
Allen, Laurie
Allen, Rick (see HEAVY METAL)
Allison, Jerry
Appice, Carmine
Appice, Vinnie
Avory, Mick

B

Bachman, Robbie
Badanjek, John
Bailey, Keith
Baker, Ginger
Barbata, John
Barlow, Barriemore
Beard, Frank
Below, Fred
Bennett, Brian
Berg, Ron
Bevan, Bev
Bidwell, Dave
Black, Jimmy Carl
Black, Jet (see NEW WAVE)
Bonham, John
Bouchard, Albert (see HEAVY METAL)
Boudreaux, John
Bozzio, Terry
Britton, Geoff
Bruford, Bill
Buckler, Rick (see NEW WAVE)
Budgie (see NEW WAVE)
Bunker, Clive
Burgess, Richard
Burke, Clem (see NEW WAVE)
Burr, Clive (see HEAVY METAL)
Buttrey, Kenny

C

Caldwell, Bobby
Cann, Warren (See NEW WAVE)
Capaldi, Jim
Cassidy, Ed
Cattini, Clem
Chambers, Martin (see NEW WAVE)
Chancler, Ndugu Leon
Clarke, Michael
Clifford, Doug
Cobham, Billy
Collins, Phil
Colomby, Bobby
Conway, Gerry
Cook, Paul (see NEW WAVE)
Cooper, Ray
Copeland, Stewart
Coughlan, John
Coughlan, Richard
Cox, Terry
Criss, Peter
Cuffley, John

D

Davies, Cliff
Davison, Brian
De Freitas, Pete (see NEW WAVE)
De Vitto, Liberty
Densmore, John
Dharma, Ritchie
Downey, Brian
Dryden, Spencer
Dunbar, Aynsley
Dunbar, Sly

E

Earl, Roger
Elliott, Bobby
Elliott, Dennis
English, Joe
Erskine, Pete

F

Fleetwood, Mick
Fontana, D. J.

G

Gary, Bruce
Giles, Mike
Gill, Frank (see HEAVY METAL)
Glockler, Nigel (see HEAVY METAL)
Gordon, Jim
Gratzner, Alan
Guerin, John

H

Hart, Mickey
Hartley, Keef
Hartman, John
Hawkins, Roger
Hayward, Ritchie
Headon, Topper (see NEW WAVE)
Helm, Levon
Henley, Don
Henrit, Bob
Heyman, Preston
Hiseman, Jon
Holland, Dave
Hooper, Stix
Hugg, Mike
Humphrey, Ralph

I

Isidore, Conrad
Isidore, Reg

J

Jackson, Al
Johnson, Jaimo
Jones, Kenny

K

Kerslake, Lee
King, Simon
Kirke, Simon
Kits, Drum
Knudsen, Keith
Kramer, Joey (see HEAVY METAL)
Kreutzman, Bill (see Mickey Hart)
Kunkel, Russ

L

Laff, Mark (see NEW WAVE)
Laing, Corky
Lamble, Martin
Lavis, Gilson
Lear, Graham
Lee, Ric
Liebezeit, Jaki
Lordan, Bill
Lynch, Stan

M

Marotta, Jerry
Marshall, John
Mason, Nick
Mattacks, Dave
McBrain, Nico (see HEAVY METAL)
McCracken, Chet (see Keith Knudsen)
McCulloch, Andy
McIntosh, Robbie
McKenna, Ted
Miles, Buddy
Mitchell, Mitch
Modeliste, Ziggy
Morlen, Pierre
Moon, Keith
Moore, Gil
Moreira, Airto
Morganstein, Rod
Moseley, Ian
Mouzon, Alphonse

N

Newman, Tony
Nicol, Steve (see NEW WAVE)

O

Oldaker, Jamie
Olsson, Nigel

P

Paice, Ian
Palmer, Carl
Palmer, Earl
Parker, Andy (see HEAVY
    METAL)
Parnell, Ric
Parry, Steve (see NEW WAVE)
Parsons, Gene
Peart, Neil
Phillips, Simon
Porcaro, Jeff
Pope, Roger
Powell, Alan (see Simon King)
Powell, Cozy
Prince, Viv
Purdie, Bernard
Pyle, Pip

R

Ramone, Tommy (see NEW
    WAVE)
Rowland, Bruce
Rudd, Phil (see HEAVY
    METAL)

S

Scabies, Rat (see NEW WAVE)
Schwarzenberg, Allan
Seraphine, Daniel
Shearer, John
Shirley, Jerry
Shrieve, Mike
Slade, Chris
Smith, Steve
Spevock, Ed
Spinetti, Henry
Starr, Ringo
Sweet, Darrell

T

Taylor, Phil (see HEAVY
    METAL)
Taylor, Roger
Thompson, Chester
Thompson, Paul
Townsend, Rob
Trucks, Butch (see Jaimo
    Johnson)
Tucker, Maureen
Twink

U

Underwood, Mick

V

Van Der Linden, Pierre
Van Halen, Alex (see
    HEAVY METAL)
Vander, Christian
Vitale, Joe

W

Walden, Narada Michael
Wallace, Ian
Waller, Micky
Ward, Andy
Ward, Bill
Watts, Charlie
Weathers, John
Weinberg, Max
White, Alan
White, Maurice
Williams, Terry
Williams, Tony
Wilson, B. J.
Withers, Pick
Wyatt, Robert

Y

York, Pete

Z

Zehringer, Randy

Dylan, Bob	Ian Wallace

E

Eagles, The	Don Henley
Earth, Wind and Fire	Maurice White
Earth	Bill Ward
Eclection	Gerry Conway
Electric Flag	Buddy Miles
Electric Light Orchestra	Bev Bevan
Eleventh House	Alphonse Mouzon
Emerson, Lake and Palmer	Carl Palmer
Energy	Ginger Baker
Episode Six	Mick Underwood
Every Which Way	Brian Davison
Eyes Of Blue	John Weathers

F

Faces, The	Kenny Jones
Factory, The	Ritchie Hayward
Fairport Convention	Bruce Rowland
	Dave Mattacks
	Martin Lamble
Fame, Georgie	Jon Hiseman
Family	Rob Townsend
Ferris Wheel	Dennis Elliott
Firefall	Michael Clarke
Fleetwood Mac	Mick Fleetwood
Flying Burrito Brothers	Gene Parsons
	Michael Clarke
Focus	Colin Allen
	Pierre Van Der Linden
Foghat	Roger Earl
Foreigner	Dennis Elliott
Formerly Fat Harry	Laurie Allen
Fotheringay	Gerry Conway
Frampton, Peter	Jamie Oldaker
Fraternity Of Man	Ritchie Hayward
Free	Simon Kirke

G

Gabriel, Peter	Jerry Marotta
Genesis	Chester Thompson
	Phil Collins
Gentle Giant	John Weathers
Georgie Fame and the Blue Flames	Mitch Mitchell
Geronimo Black	Jimmy Carl Black
Giants, The	Bruce Gary
Gillan	Mick Underwood
Gillespie, Dana	Simon Phillips
Ginger Baker's Airforce	Alan White
Gods, The	Lee Kerslake
Golliwogs, The	Doug Clifford
Gong	Laurie Allen
	Pierre Moerlen
Gonzalez	Preston Heyman
Graham Bond Initiation	Keith Bailey
Graham Bond Organisation	Ginger Baker
	Jon Hiseman
Grateful Dead, The	Bill Kreutzman (see Mickey Hart)
Grease Band, The	Bruce Rowland
Greenslade	Andrew McCulloch
Grimes, Carol	Preston Heyman

Gryphon	Alan White

H

Hackett, Steve	John Shearer
Hall & Oates	Jerry Marotta
Hammer	Cozy Powell
Happy Magazine	Alan White
Hardin & York	Pete York
Hart, Mickey	Grateful Dead
Hatfield and The North	Pip Pyle
Hawkwind	Ginger Baker
	Simon King
	Alan Powell (see Simon King)
Heavy Metal	Rick Allen
	Albert Bouchard
	Clive Burr
	Frank Gill
	Nigel Glockler
	Hoey Kramer
	Nico McBrain
	Andy Parker
	Phil Rudd
	Phil Taylor
	Alex Van Halen
Hendrix, Jimi	Buddy Miles
Herd, The	Mick Underwood
	Henry Spinetti
Hollies, The	Bobby Elliott
Holy Magick	John Weathers
Hookfoot	Roger Pope
Humble Pie	Jerry Shirley
Hummingbird	Bernard Purdie
	Conrad Isidore
Hunter Ronson	Denis Elliott
Hustler	Henry Spinetti

I

If	Cliff Davies
	Dennis Elliott
In Crowd, The	Twink

J

Jack Bruce Band	Bruce Gary
Jefferson Airplane	John Barbata
	Spencer Dryden
Jefferson Starship	Aynsley Dunbar
Jethro Tull	Barriemore Barlow
	Clive Bunker
Jimi Hendrix Experience	Mitch Mitchell
Joel Billy	Ray Cooper
John, Elton	Nigel Olsson
	Roger Pope
John Mayall's Bluesbreakers	Aynsley Dunbar
	Colin Allen
	Mick Fleetwood
	Jon Hiseman
	Keef Hartley
Journey	Aynsley Dunbar
	Steve Smith
Judas Jump	Henry Spinetti
Judas Priest	Dave Holland
Jude	Clive Bunker

K

KGB	Carmine Appice
Kiki Dee Band	Roger Pope
King Crimson	Andrew McCulloch
	Bill Bruford
	Ian Wallace
	Jamie Muir
	Mike Giles
Kinks, The	Mick Avory
Kiss	Peter Criss
Knack, The	Bruce Gary

L

Lake, Greg	Ted McKenna
Landscape	Richard Burgess
Led Zeppelin	John Bonham
Lifetime	Tony Williams
Little Feat	Ritchie Hayward

M

Magma	Christian Vander
Mahavishnu Orchestra	Billy Cobham
	Narada Michael Walden
Man	Terry Williams
Manfred Mann's Earthband	Chris Slade
Mann, Manfred	Mike Hugg
Mar-Keys, The	Al Jackson
Matching Mole	Robert Wyatt
May Blitz	Tony Newman
McCoys, The	Randy Zehringer
Meters, The	Ziggy Modeliste
Michael Schenker Band	Cozy Powell
Mitch Ryder and the Detroit Wheels	John Badanjek
Mitchell, Joni	John Guerin
Montrose, Ronnie	Steve Smith
Moon	John Shearer
Mountain	Corky Laing
Move, The	Bev Bevan
Muscle Shoals Rhythm Section	Roger Hawkins

N

National Health	Pip Pyle
National Head Band	Lee Kerslake
Natural Gas	Jerry Shirley
Nazareth	Darrell Sweet
Neutrons, The	John Weathers
New Riders Of The Purple Sage	Spencer Dryden
New Wave	Jet Black
	Rick Buckler
	Budgie
	Clem Burke
	Warren Cann
	Martin Chambers
	Paul Cook
	Pete De Freitas
	Topper Headon
	Mark Laff
	Steve Parry
	Tommy Ramone
New York	Pete York

Nice, The	Brian Davison
Nugent, Ted	Cliff Davies

O

P

Outlaws, The	Mick Underwood

P.M.	Carl Palmer
Paice, Ashton & Lord	Ian Paice
Paramounts, The	B. J. Wilson
Paraphernalia	Jon Hiseman
Pat Travers Band	Tommy Aldridge
Peace	Mick Underwood
Pentangle	Terry Cox
Phoenix	Rob Henrit
Piblokto	John Weathers
Pink Fairies, The	Twink
Pink Floyd	Nick Mason
Plastic Ono Band	Alan White
Police	Stewart Copeland
Ponty, Jean Luc	Steve Smith
Presley, Elvis	D. J. Fontana
Pretty Things, The	Twink
	Viv Prince
	Mitch Mitchell
Procol Harum	B. J. Wilson

Q

Queen	Roger Taylor

R

REO Speedwagon	Alan Gratzer
Rainbow	Cozy Powell
Refugee	Brian Davison
Return To Forever	Airto Moreira
Riot Squad, The	Mitch Mitchell
Rockets, The	John Badanjek
Rockpile	Terry Williams
Rolling Stones, The	Charlie Watts
Ronnie Lane's Slim Chance	Bruce Rowland
Rough Diamond	Geoff Britton
Roxy Music	Paul Thompson
Roy Young Band	Cliff Davies
Rush	Airto Moreira

S

Santana	Airto Moreira
	Graham Lear
	Mike Shrieve
	Ndugu Leon Chancler
Savoy Brown	Dave Bidwell
	Roger Earl
Seal Level	Joe English
Section, The	Russ Kunkel
Seger, Bob	Jamie Oldaker
Sensational Alex Harvey Band	Red McKenna
Shadows, The	Brian Bennett
Shiloh	Don Henley
Shotgun Express	Mick Fleetwood
Small Faces, The	Kenny Jones
Snape	Ian Wallace
Soft Machine	John Marshall

Sorcerers	Robert Wyatt
Soul Agents, The	Cozy Powell
Soul Giants, The	Roger Pope
Sounds Incorporated	Jimmy Carl Black
Souther Hillman Furay Band	Tony Newman
Spencer Davis Group	Jim Gordon
	Nigel Olsson
	Pete York
Spirit	Ed Cassidy
Springsteen, Bruce	Max Weinberg
Squeeze	Gilson Lavis
Status Quo	John Coughlan
Steamhammer	Micky Waller
Steampacket	Micky Waller
Steve Stills Band	Russ Kunkel
Stevens, Cat	Gerry Conway
Stewart, Rod	Colin Allen
	Carmine Appice
Stomu Yamashta's go	Mike Shrieve
Stone The Crows	Colin Allen
Strange Brew	Cozy Powell
Strapps	Mick Underwood
Stray Gators	John Barbata
	Kenny Buttrey
Streetwalkers	Ian Wallace

Tandoori Cassette	Barriemore Barlow
Teargas	Ted McKenna
Tempest	Jon Hiseman
Ten Years After	Ric Lee
The Crazy World Of Arthur Brown	Carl Palmer
The Rockers	Carmine Appice
Thin Lizzy	Brian Downey
Toefat	Lee Kerslake
Tom Petty and the Heartbreakers	Stan Lynch
Tommy Bolin Band	Narada Michael Walden
Tomorrow	Twink
Tornadoes, The	Clem Cattini
Toto	Jeff Porcaro
Traffic	Jim Capaldi
Trapeze	Dave Holland
Troops	Roger Pope
Trower, Robin	Reg Isidore
	Bill Lordan
Tundra	Henry Spinetti
Turtles, The	John Barbata

U.K.	Bill Bruford
	Terry Bozzio
Uriah Heep	Chris Slade
	Lee Kerslake
	Nigel Olsson

V

Vanilla Fudge	Carmine Appice
Velvet Underground, The	Maureen Tucker

Warriors, The	Ian Wallace
Weather Report	Alphonse Mouzon
	Chester Thompson
	Ndugu Leon Chancler
	Pete Erskine
West, Bruce & Laing	Corky Laing
Whitesnake	Ian Paice
Who, The	Keith Moon
	Kenny Jones
Wilcox, Toyah	Simon Phillips
Wilde Flowers	Richard Coughlan
	Robert Wyatt
Wings	Geoff Britton
	Joe English
Winter, Johnny	Bobby Caldwell
	Randy Zehringer
Wolf	John Shearer

Yes	Alan White
	Bill Bruford

Z

Z. Z. Top	Frank Beard
Zappa, Frank	John Guerin
	Terry Bozzio
	Aynsley Dunbar
	Jimmy Carl Black
	Chester Thompson
	Ralph Humphrey
Zoot Money's Big Roll Band	Colin Allen